Forgiveness and Reconciliation

in the aftermath of abuse

The Faith and Order Commission

CHURCH HOUSE
PUBLISHING

The Faith and Order Commission began working on the area of theology and safeguarding in 2014, in response to a request from the lead bishop for safeguarding to the House of Bishops' Standing Committee for theological material that could complement what was being produced by the National Safeguarding Team in terms of policy and training. This is the second of two texts produced by the Faith and Order Commission to meet that request, the first, *The Gospel, Sexual Abuse and the Church*, having been published in 2016. It has been approved for publication and commended for study by the House of Bishops.

William Nye
Secretary to the House of Bishops
September 2017

Church House Publishing
Church House
Great Smith Street
London SW1P 3AZ

ISBN 978 0 7151 1132 1

Published 2017 for the Faith and Order Commission
of the Church of England by Church House Publishing

Indexes by Meg Davies
Typeset by ForDesign
Printed by CPI Group (UK) Ltd

Contents

Preface by the Rt Revd Christopher Cocksworth,
    Chair of the Faith and Order Commission   6
Summary   9
Introduction   17

PART I: UNDERSTANDING ABUSE   31
1.   What do we mean by 'abuse'?   32
2.   What is distinctive about abuse as a form of sin?   41

PART II: RESPONDING TO ABUSE   53
3.   Is there a place for repentance by churches where
    they have shared in some way in the sin of abuse?   54
    Fictional Case Study: St Matthew's   65
4.   How should the church speak of being forgiven
    to those who have committed abuse?   70
    Fictional Case Study: David   82
5.   How should the church speak of forgiving to those
    who have experienced abuse?   85
    Fictional Case Study: Darren   98
6.   Does the church have a ministry of reconciliation
    in the aftermath of abuse?   101
    Fictional Case Study: Andrew and Jody   112
Conclusion   115

Notes   118
Subject Index   123
Index of biblical citations   127

Preface

For the past three years, the Faith and Order Commission has been engaged in preparing some substantial resources for thinking theologically about the challenges faced by the Church of England – alongside other churches – in preventing abuse and in responding well where it has happened. This work has been undertaken in careful consultation with those responsible for safeguarding at the national level in the Church of England, and with the House of Bishops. It has already resulted in the publication of *The Gospel, Sexual Abuse and the Church: A Theological Resource for the Local Church* (Church House Publishing, 2016), and I am very pleased that this concise, accessible text is being widely read and used in the church.

In a couple of places, *The Gospel, Sexual Abuse and the Church* refers to another document to be published by the Faith and Order Commission: *Forgiveness and Reconciliation in the Aftermath of Abuse*. In agreeing to address this subject, the Commission was always aware that it would face some significant difficulties. It is, to a considerable extent, new ground: while much has been written about each of these three things – forgiveness, reconciliation and the aftermath of abuse – there is not a great deal that addresses them together in the way that is attempted in this document. At the same time, this is territory that for survivors potentially touches on matters of deep hurt, including in some cases hurt for which those claiming to represent the church bear a primary responsibility.

Yet neither is it territory that the church can simply avoid. At some point in the aftermath of abuse, people who want to affirm the good news of new life in Christ are likely to ask, in one way or another, 'How does forgiveness, human and divine, relate to this situation? How does reconciliation, human and divine, relate to this situation? And what might the hope for forgiveness and reconciliation have to do with the need for justice, human and divine, in the face of this sin, this crime?' Wrong and misleading answers to these questions have been too common in the churches and in some cases have done much damage, which is why we have focused on them. That is not to say, of course, that there are no other critical theological questions raised by the challenges of preventing and responding well to abuse.

Forgiveness and Reconciliation in the Aftermath of Abuse is particularly intended to provide guidance for all those who preach, teach and exercise pastoral ministry in the Church of England. Whether or not we are conscious of it, much if not most public ministry will be exercised 'in the aftermath of abuse' so far as some of those receiving it are concerned. In preparing it, the Faith and Order Commission was very conscious both of the need to balance different and at times contrasting perspectives, and of the interrelationship between its different parts. We would want to encourage readers to take account of the text as a whole in seeking to interpret and learn from specific sections. The initial summary is designed to help with this by providing something of a map to navigate around the document.

I would like to record my gratitude to the members of the previous and current Faith and Order Commission for their work on this document, as also to those who have assisted it in its work, some as part of the

drafting group and others as commentators on successive revisions.
I would especially want to thank those survivors of abuse who
contributed to this process in various ways, without whose help
this project could not have been considered, let alone completed.

The Rt Revd Dr Christopher Cocksworth
Bishop of Coventry
Chair of the Faith and Order Commission

June 2017

Summary

While forgiveness and reconciliation are central themes in the church's proclamation of the gospel, teaching in this area has sometimes been unbalanced and badly formulated, with serious consequences for Christian ministry to survivors and perpetrators of abuse, and for the church's witness to wider society. Superficial understandings of forgiveness, opposing it to justice, lead to destructive expectations of those who have been sinned against; weak understandings of repentance, which disconnect it from justice and the restoration of right relationships, fail to offer sinners the good news of Jesus Christ. Understanding the gravity of sin leads us to see both the astonishing abundance of God's grace in forgiveness, and the profound transformations that are needed as we walk the way of repentance.

This document aims, first, to address specific challenges to the church as it seeks to speak truthfully in the aftermath of abuse about forgiveness and reconciliation, which are inseparable from repentance and justice, and second, to provide material to help dioceses and parishes who find themselves facing that reality. Every person licensed to preach and teach in the life of the Church of England needs to be aware that whenever they speak about forgiveness to a congregation or group of people within it, it is entirely possible that a survivor, or an abuser, may be present. The issues raised here are therefore also relevant to all of us whose ministry is exercised 'in the aftermath of abuse' on many occasions, and often without our direct knowledge.

The text addresses six related questions. They could have been asked in a different order; in particular, since the declared policy of the Church of

England in responding to abuse is to keep victims and survivors central, there is an obvious case for saying that the question directly relating to survivors should come first. Yet part of what the subgroup who worked on the document heard from survivors was that forgiveness is by no means the first word that survivors generally wish to hear from the church, either as a demand from them or as an offer to those who abused them. Indeed, for some survivors there is real anger that the church seems so preoccupied with forgiveness in the aftermath of abuse, when the focus should be on justice. Before turning to the pivotal question of how the church should speak with those who have experienced abuse about forgiving those who have wronged them, this document therefore addresses problems with the church's acknowledgement of its own failures in preventing and responding to abuse, and the question of what it should be saying about forgiveness to those who have committed abuse.

Of the six questions that frame the document, the first two concern the understanding of abuse within a theological framework, and the remaining four then focus on the place of forgiveness and reconciliation in the church's response to abuse. The questions are:

1.   What do we mean by 'abuse'?
2.   What is distinctive about abuse as a form of sin?
3.   Is there a place for repentance by churches when they have shared in some way in the sin of abuse?
4.   How should the church speak of being forgiven to those who have committed abuse?
5.   How should the church speak of forgiving to those who have experienced abuse?

6.   Does the church have a ministry of reconciliation in the aftermath of abuse?

What do we mean by 'abuse'? Some will think immediately of various forms of sexual abuse, though many other forms of abuse exist. Reflection on the harrowing biblical story of the rape of Tamar in 2 Samuel 13 suggests four characteristic dimensions that can apply across this range: (i) serious harm on the part of the victim; made possible by (ii) an imbalance of power between victim and perpetrator; linked to (iii) the perpetrator's position of trust; and abetted by (iv) deceit on the perpetrator's behalf, denying what has happened and making others more or less witting accomplices.

What is distinctive about abuse as a form of sin? The sin of abuse can have far-reaching and highly destructive effects on the person who suffers it: effects which last for a long time and affect many relationships, including the human–divine relationship. Recovery from abuse can be long, complicated and difficult. Memories may surface in an unexpected and distressing manner, and the emotional response to what is recalled may differ over time. For the abuser, abuse distorts the will and corrupts the conscience. Moreover, abuse may be the occasion which draws into sin others who hold responsibility in the relevant institution and society for ensuring that justice is done and seen to be done. Those who become aware of abuse may fail to respond appropriately and so compound the sin, for example by denying or concealing the abuse, or by giving way to hatred and vengeance. This failure undermines the work of the justice which is achieved by the public, effective and visible work of the government, law and statutory authorities charged with prosecuting injustice without fear or favour. This 'temporal' justice is commissioned by God to do its work and is of immense value to society, especially to victims of abuse. Accordingly, it should be held in high esteem by the Church of England, and especially by those who hold responsibility within it.

Is there a place for repentance by churches when they have shared in some way in the sin of abuse? The church as the body of Christ has sometimes failed to respond with justice and compassion for the abused when its members have committed sins of abuse. It needs to acknowledge its part in compounding those sins and change its ways. It also needs to work out its relationship with those who have suffered on account of the naivety, negligence and complicity that have let the church become an arena of abuse. Apology may well be required but in a Christian context cannot be separated from the call to repentance. Like all repentance, this cannot be achieved merely by words or gestures, but needs to be a thoroughgoing change of attitude, thinking and behaviour. The concept of ecclesial repentance is significant here and should be carefully considered by the Church of England. One critical question that needs to be faced is how far weak or misleading doctrine has contributed to the church's failings in preventing and responding to abuse. A false opposition between forgiveness and justice would be one example of this.

How should the church speak of being forgiven to those who have committed abuse? God's offer of forgiveness through the cross of Christ is for all; none has the slightest claim or entitlement to it in light of their merits, and for each it opens up the way to transformation beyond any imagining. That is the good news, and it is the joyful duty of the church to proclaim it. Turning to God to receive forgiveness also means turning away from the wrong we have done, and recognizing it as sin that separates us from God and one another and binds us to death. Responding to God's offer of salvation therefore involves repentance as well as boundless thankfulness. In the case of those who have committed abuse, part of such repentance will be a willingness to face the consequences, including legal consequences, of acknowledging the sin that has been committed. This has implications for the ministry of absolution within the church. Moreover, the nature of abuse (and not least the way it may habituate the abuser to self-deceit) can make it difficult for repentance to take root. Evidence of repentance cannot mean that no constraints should be placed on a person's access to situations where re-offending would be possible.

How should the church speak of forgiving to those who have experienced abuse? The church's primary pastoral task is to listen with care and sensitivity to those who have been abused, supporting them on the road towards healing and in taking steps towards the achievement of temporal justice. Christian ministers should avoid the use of trivializing language about forgiveness which suggests that it is easy, instant or a condition of God's continued love. The words on forgiveness in the Lord's Prayer need to be read as the prayer of the whole church, seeking to be like the Father through the Son in the power of the Spirit, not asserting a claim on God's forgiveness based on our individual performance of it. In real life, forgiveness is rarely a straightforward exchange between victim and perpetrator in which complete repentance is met by complete forgiveness. Rather than being an episode or an event, forgiving is better understood as a long journey or struggle with the claims of justice and mercy, during the course of which forgiveness emerges.

Does the church have a ministry of reconciliation in the aftermath of abuse? Reconciliation has many dimensions. One expression of reconciliation is the face-to-face meeting of the people involved. The hope of ultimate reconciliation in Christ is a distinctive hope of the church, but the implied resumption of relationship with the abuser can be disturbing for those who have suffered traumatic and shattering consequences of abuse and is certainly not something that should be forced on a survivor of abuse. Any intentional steps towards some kind of formal reconciliation, including (in this context) various forms of restorative practice, must be fully respectful of the survivor of abuse and their wishes. For all the challenges here, there will be cases where movement towards reconciliation may be possible. They are most likely to be situations where temporal justice has been exercised, healing is a reality for the abused, and the abuser's repentance leads to reform. The church's ministry of reconciliation in the aftermath of abuse is primarily demonstrated in seeking for these things, rather than in facilitating the reconciliation process as such, especially when the church has been involved in the abuse in some way.

This document is written to be read as a whole, with answers to earlier questions providing essential material for those that follow. It will be best understood as a whole. Nonetheless, this summary, and cross-references within the text, should enable those who have a specific interest in one of the questions to focus on that. Others may prefer to begin with Part II and refer back to Part I as needed.

As a text from the Faith and Order Commission, *Forgiveness and Reconciliation in the Aftermath of Abuse* is primarily intended to address theological issues that arise from the practice of Christian ministry and thereby strengthen preaching, teaching and public communication by the church. It should be read alongside *The Gospel, Sexual Abuse and the Church: A Theological Resource for the Local Church*, also from the Faith and Order Commission, which addresses the wider context of safeguarding in the life of the church.

It must also be read alongside the Church of England's extensive practice guidance for safeguarding, and it in no way replaces it or substitutes for it, or indeed for proper professional consultation. Readers may however value some indication of the range of situations in which these theological issues can arise and how they relate to decisions about action by churches and those with positions of responsibility in them. In the second part of the document, 'Responding to Abuse', a brief fictional case study follows each main section to help stimulate reflection and discussion on these matters.

Introduction

Origin and purpose of the document

This document is one of two texts from the Faith and Order Commission intended to contribute towards theological thinking within the Church of England about its response to abuse. Such response extends from safeguarding work and pastoral care of survivors at parish level, to preaching and teaching about related issues and to public statements from church representatives that may elicit immediate attention from national media.

These texts originated in discussions within the House of Bishops and elsewhere that identified both a critical and a constructive theological task. The critical task is to identify areas where mistaken theological ideas may be invoked to inform responses to abuse that cause harm to people. The constructive task is to outline some of the ways in which the great riches of theology, including practical theology in its engagement with the human sciences, can be drawn on to inform responses that are life-giving and theologically truthful. Both documents are offered as contributions to the ongoing work of theological thinking about the churches' response to abuse, work that will continue to require energy and attention at many levels, and not as definitive statements or authoritative reports.

The companion document from the Faith and Order Commission to this one, *The Gospel, Sexual Abuse and the Church: A Theological Resource for the Local Church*, is designed to be read and used by the widest possible range of people who carry responsibility within the life of the

Church of England for safeguarding from abuse and for responding to survivors. It focuses specifically on issues raised by sexual abuse and draws in a wide range of theological themes. By contrast, this document is concerned to attend to abuse in its different forms, not all of them sexual, while dealing with the critical theological themes of forgiveness and reconciliation – bearing in mind from the outset that there are important questions about the relationship between these two themes and that they are not simply two ways of saying the same thing. It is hoped that there will be valuable material in it for all who want to engage with the work of theological thinking about the churches' response to abuse, but it is written with two specific aims in mind.

The first is to offer some general guidance to those who preach and teach as to how the theological themes of forgiveness and reconciliation may relate to the lives of people who have been involved in abuse in some way. It may be helpful to think of four broad types of involvement here: those who have suffered abuse, those who have committed abuse, those who hold responsibilities for preventing and dealing with abuse, and the broader category of 'bystanders' who become aware of cases of abuse in one way or another. There is always a reasonable chance that a congregation will include people from some or all of these categories, which are not mutually exclusive. The first, those who have suffered abuse, is the most critical, as there is real potential to do further damage through poor doctrinal understanding and inadequate expression. The second aim is to provide theological resources for those who may be called upon to represent the Church of England in speaking publicly in the aftermath of abuse. This would include high-profile cases where bishops may be involved, but it would also include situations where someone needs to say something to the local congregation and perhaps to the local media about a case of abuse that has become known, whether alleged or proven, and that relates to church officers or members. The document is not designed to provide off-the-peg material for use in such situations, but to assist in the careful, prayerful and theologically responsible reflection that should be part of the process wherever possible.

Inevitably, there are significant areas of overlap between the territory covered in the document and other very serious situations that face the church. Parallel issues would also be likely to arise, for instance around the meaning of forgiveness in the context of families coming to terms with the murder of a family member, or of whole communities recovering from violent conflict. The hope would be that there could be some material of value here for those seeking to minister in such contexts, without blurring the differences between these situations.

Types of abuse

The understanding of the phenomenon of abuse presented here was guided by the framework of national church policy on the safeguarding of children and adults. This framework is informed by the UK government document *Working Together*, which distinguishes four primary types of abuse in the case of children: physical, sexual, emotional and neglect.[1] While in popular usage 'child abuse' can be heard as presupposing sexual activity, this wider frame of reference is fundamental for approaches to safeguarding in the statutory and voluntary sectors. Church of England policy documents draw on this fourfold classification but supplement it in various ways, not least because they also address abuse of adults, including domestic abuse.[2] Cases of abuse that come to attention within the context of congregational life are likely to span these different types, including domestic violence, which raises very particular challenges when both partners are members of the same congregation.

At various points, these policy documents also speak of other types of abuse, including spiritual,[3] cultural, ritual and digital abuse.[4] These terms, along with others such as institutional abuse, name ways in which aspects of the shared context of abuser and abused become connected with abuse, thereby both sustaining the space for abusers to operate and negatively shaping the experience of those abused at multiple levels. Spiritual abuse, where the perpetrator deploys spiritual language as part of the coercion of those abused and the justification for their actions, is a particularly significant feature to be kept in mind when considering abuse within church communities. While by no means restricted to those holding formal office, it nonetheless raises important and challenging issues about the behaviour of those carrying high levels of responsibility in the church, including clergy, and the ways in which these can be exercised to invoke supposed spiritual authority in order to do real spiritual harm to others.

The report seeks to address the range of contexts in which people are abused. Abuse is the exploitation of interpersonal or institutional power, and often has far-reaching consequences for those who are abused, as well as for the wider community. The range of abuse is huge and no abstract overarching analysis can be offered here. Responses to the two questions in the first part of the document attempt to provide an account of abuse that corresponds with the Church of England's policy statements and with general usage, while also exploring what might be said to characterize abuse as sin from the different points of view of those involved. The aim here is to provide a framework that can help us to address the questions in the second part about how the church responds to abuse. What might forgiveness and reconciliation mean in the aftermath of this particular kind of sin?

Forgiveness and reconciliation in contemporary context

Forgiveness and reconciliation have become subjects of extensive discussion in popular and academic circles alike over the last couple of decades. Forgiveness has become a huge subject of both study and therapeutic application in the psychological world, while philosophical ethicists and theologians have begun to turn their minds to the difficult problems of interpersonal forgiveness which many in the life of the church (including those with positions of leadership and public representation) assume to be straightforward.[5] 'Forgiveness Studies' is an emerging area of serious academic and applied multi-disciplinary work. Interest in forgiveness ranges from the work of specialized units at numerous American universities to the concern of many a journalist after a political murder.

There are also substantial recent theological resources to help understand forgiveness. L. Gregory Jones' *Embodying Forgiveness* and Miroslav Volf's *Exclusion and Embrace* were published just as this theme was awaking from a long hibernation, and they still have much to say.[6] Significant studies since then would include *Forgiveness and Christian Ethics* by Anthony Bash and *Healing Agony* by Stephen Cherry.[7]

Although widely seen as a 'Christian word', however, this newfound interest in forgiveness has not, in the main, been driven by the church (with the exception of the widespread influence of Archbishop Desmond Tutu).[8] Indeed, for many the pious, religious and theological overtones with which the word 'forgiveness' has become associated are problematic. Donald Shriver has written about the 'sacramental captivity of forgiveness',[9] and in the preface of a recently published book about the well-known Forgiveness Project, Marian Partington (whose sister was incarcerated, abused and killed by the Wests of Gloucester) is quoted, saying that forgiveness has been 'barnacled by aeons of piety'.[10]

Across these various contexts, people may use the term 'forgiveness' in significantly different ways. We might distinguish between two broad paradigms for forgiveness, which can be encountered in relatively 'pure' forms or blended together in various ways. On the one hand there is a paradigm of 'therapeutic' forgiveness, in which forgiving is primarily for the benefit of the person who has been hurt, and does not require any actual contact with the person who hurt them. On the other hand there is a paradigm of 'interpersonal' forgiveness, associated for instance with New Testament teaching, and the focus of interest in forgiveness in philosophical ethics, where forgiving is done primarily for the benefit of the person who has sinned, and therefore implies some exchange between those who give and receive forgiveness. The paradoxical language of 'forgiving oneself', for instance (which appears in the fictional case study at the end of section 5 below), makes more sense where the implicit paradigm is therapeutic forgiveness. The material that follows focuses on interpersonal forgiveness, without wishing to imply any devaluing of the healing process that is central to therapeutic approaches.

Similarly, reconciliation has come to receive extensive attention, not least in the church in general and in the Anglican context in particular, where it is seen as a word which offers a variety of meanings, ranging from an aspiration for peaceful cohabitation of those with differing beliefs and theologies within one church, to a mode of continued communal struggle which stops short of becoming violent.

In the midst of this great variety of creative work, there are different views about the relationship between forgiveness and reconciliation. The idea that they are inextricably connected came to prominence through the influence of Archbishop Tutu in the Truth and Reconciliation process in South Africa. Since then, the study of both forgiveness and reconciliation has moved on with extraordinary energy, and it is now more common for scholars and writers to consider the difference between the two.[11] Certainly in the experience of many survivors of abuse, the two concepts need to be kept separate.

The relationship between forgiveness and repentance has also received considerable attention. Philosophers and psychologists as well as theologians have discussed whether repentance precedes or follows forgiveness, and whether repentance is even necessary for forgiveness.[12] As will become apparent, this is a critical question for the contexts being considered here.

When it addresses questions of forgiveness and reconciliation, therefore, the church is touching on the personal struggles of many survivors of abuse, and also on nuanced, subtle matters which are the subject of active, ongoing cultural and academic discussion. While the answers to the questions in Part II seek to be informed by such an awareness, the present document does not offer a survey of current literature on this topic or a critical evaluation of it. The focus is on relating what the sources of Christian theology have to say about repentance, forgiveness and reconciliation to the particular and challenging issues that confront the church when it responds to the aftermath of abuse. While it may be tempting to think that the familiar language of forgiveness and being forgiven can be applied straightforwardly to the human realities we are facing when children or adults have been abused, or, by contrast, that it simply has no purchase on them, the truth is that those realities demand that we think through the full implications of our theology of forgiveness with renewed honesty and discipline.

The place of justice

One of the most pressing questions in the minds of those who suffer abuse – and sometimes even those who perpetrate it – is the question of justice. Forgiveness, reconciliation and justice do stand, to some extent, in theological tension,[13] yet it can never be right to set them in opposition, as if we have to choose between forgiveness and justice. Holding forgiveness, reconciliation and justice in a properly balanced tension is a significant part of the task of formulating a theology that can inform the work of safeguarding from abuse, and responding to it.

Since this is a theme that will recur with some frequency in this document, it will be useful to introduce some clarifications at this stage. In discussing the place of justice in the life of the church generally, and in relation to forgiveness and reconciliation in particular, four related senses of 'justice' can be distinguished: (1) justice as a state of affairs in which there are right relations between people; (2) temporal justice as a work of judgement to be done in some circumstances when right relations are harmed, such as in cases of abuse; (3) justice as a virtue; and (4) eschatological justice as God's final judgement.[14]

Any theological account of justice must be rooted in the right relations that God intended for humanity from creation, the good way of life that the Book of Genesis describes in the time of humanity's innocence, when injustice did not mark human relations. Justice in this sense might be best understood as a state of affairs in which the equal worth of each human being within the created order is honoured.[15] In the aftermath of sin, this worth was reaffirmed in the covenant made and law given to Israel and fulfilled through Christ's incarnation, ministry, death, resurrection and ascension. For humanity now, this worth grounds certain obligations of love towards others which all should keep. Abuse is an example of the failure to keep these obligations, a failure to treat people according to their worth in the eyes of God as revealed in Christ. Justice as right relations is the ground for all thinking about what it means for individuals and institutions to 'do justly' in response to abuse. The church, following Christ, has a clear responsibility to affirm that responses to abuse are to be grounded in this sense of justice as right relations, rooted in God's created order and revelation, supremely in Christ.

A fundamental task of government is to maintain a temporal order which upholds what is just and right in the relationships between people and to oppose what is unjust and wrong. It is for this purpose that government is appointed and commissioned by God: 'to punish those who do wrong and to praise those who do right' (1 Peter 2.14). This is the work of 'temporal justice' which involves doing a kind of judgement which corresponds in some way to the judgement of God, with the acknowledgement that serious failures in this work are an ever-present possibility. In this sense, temporal justice encompasses criminal and civil proceedings in the law courts, supported by the work of statutory authorities such as the police and other relevant bodies such as the prison service; it also includes the work of legislatures such as the Houses of Parliament. This justice is something that is *done* by specific temporal authorities in the making of laws and the prosecution of offences.

The church has a fundamental responsibility to assist and promote the right and proper exercise of temporal justice in every way possible. It is important to stress this given that so much of the discussion about justice in the context of abuse focuses on this sense of justice and the importance of bringing allegations of injustice speedily to the appropriate authorities. The question of how far the church's own exercise of judgement – for instance in disciplinary matters – overlaps with temporal justice as understood here is an important one; through such judgement, the church also contributes to ensuring the truth is told about abuse and action taken in the light of that truth. Distinctive features of the Church of England, such as the inclusion of ecclesiastical law as part of the law of the land and the presence of bishops in the House of Lords, would also be relevant to discussion on this issue. For the purposes of this document, however, the critical point is that while such overlap means that the church has additional processes of judgement that apply in the case of allegations of abuse, these can never be used as a replacement for the administration of temporal justice under the criminal law, or as a pretext for delaying its application.

The church's ability to fulfil its responsibility to support the work of temporal justice which pertains to government and to perform the measure of justice proper to itself can be linked to the 'virtue of justice'. Debate on this subject goes back to Plato and Aristotle. But it is clear enough that a disposition to do what is required to uphold what is just in human relationships and to oppose what is unjust can be more or less present in an individual or institution. Thus the Catechism of the Roman Catholic Church defines justice as 'the moral virtue that consists in the constant and firm will to give their due to God and neighbor'. As virtues need to be fostered in order to take root and grow in our lives, so they can also be weakened and diminished. In the aftermath of abuse, we might ask whether there was a culpable failure to practise the virtue of justice on the part of particular people or communities, for instance if the temporal justice that was 'due' in the case of someone suffering abuse had been obstructed or ignored.

Finally, the church testifies to God's 'eschatological justice' – the divine judgement that overcomes all human injustice and restores the justice of right relations that is God's will for creation. Although the original word may be the same in both Hebrew and Greek, English versions have sometimes tended to prefer 'righteousness' to 'justice' when translating passages where this meaning is clearly in view. This justice is 'eschatological' in that it relates to how God brings an *end* to the age of injustice, sin and death. For Christians, this is something God has done in Jesus Christ crucified and risen, while we also long for the fullness of that action to be made manifest and for all creation to be transformed by coming face to face with the truth that Jesus Christ is Lord. 'In accordance with his promise, we wait for new heavens and a new earth, where righteousness is at home' (2 Peter 3.13).

By prosecuting abuse and righting wrongs in a public, effective and visible manner, the work of temporal justice can provide a foretaste of this righteousness of God that is to come. In this way, the eschatological justice of God reinforces the church's motivation to honour and promote the temporal justice that is commissioned by

God to be achieved by government, courts and other relevant statutory authorities. A temptation to set at odds eschatological justice and temporal justice as if the former provided an excuse for not cooperating with the latter must be firmly resisted. This in no way excludes a role for forgiveness and reconciliation but requires that such a role be coordinated in relation to the effective working of temporal justice.

The church therefore has a specific role in relation to each of the four senses of justice that have been distinguished in this section. With regard to the first, the church calls attention to justice as the right relations between people intended by God from creation. With regard to the second, the church supports and honours the exercise of temporal justice that upholds right relationships and opposes abuse. With regard to the third, the church fosters and draws on the virtue of justice. Finally, concerning the fourth sense of justice, the church witnesses to God's eschatological justice or 'righteousness' that in turn motivates the pursuit of temporal justice in the here and now. All four senses are relevant to how the church responds in the aftermath of abuse, including any attempt it may make to speak about forgiveness and reconciliation.

PART I

Understanding Abuse

1. What do we mean by 'abuse'?

Some will think immediately of various forms of sexual abuse, though many other forms of abuse exist. Reflection on the harrowing biblical story of the rape of Tamar in 2 Samuel 13 suggests four characteristic dimensions that can apply across this range: (i) serious harm on the part of the victim; made possible by (ii) an imbalance of power between victim and perpetrator; linked to (iii) the perpetrator's position of trust; and abetted by (iv) deceit on the perpetrator's behalf, denying what has happened and making others more or less witting accomplices.

'Abuse' has been developed and explored as a central moral and legal category for our culture over the past fifty years. The range of situations to which it may be applied is diverse (perhaps increasingly so), and invoking it is a serious matter that may require a formal response. What is happening in terms of human behaviour and relationships when abuse takes place – what makes it different from other situations where people do bad things to other people?

Christian understanding is informed by the study of the Scriptures. Although the specific way our culture uses the term 'abuse' is shaped by relatively recent developments, what we are talking about here is nothing new. Scripture includes a number of passages that describe what we call 'abuse', and this and the following sections are informed by consideration of one of them, the account of the rape of Tamar by her half-brother Amnon in 2 Samuel 13.1–39.[16] This is a text that has been used for contextual Bible study on women and violence in the context of South Africa and beyond, to good effect.[17]

At the start of the narrative, Tamar's social value lies in her relationship to David and in her virginity. As Amnon knows, her position should have made her untouchable. Nevertheless, Amnon is David's first son and enjoys a favouritism that has dire consequences for Tamar. Amnon's claim to be ill means that David does not refuse his request to see Tamar and be fed by her. Amnon's position of power allows him to orchestrate the situation that enables him to rape Tamar: he sends all the servants away, thus removing a source of protection on which Tamar could rely. The narrative itself reinforces the ease with which Amnon was able to do this, as Tamar herself protests (verses 12–13).

Throughout the narrative, Tamar is treated as an object, one who can be commanded without resistance. She is summoned by David and goes to Amnon; she makes cakes, is raped and is thrown out. Her argument and pleading breaks up this pattern, but her words are ignored by Amnon. By objectifying Tamar, he gives himself the permission to treat her as less than human. The rape itself is described in objectifying terms: a literal translation might be: 'he laid her'. This refusal to acknowledge her dignity as a human person represents a fundamental denial of the claims to just treatment in accord with the right relations intended for humanity, rooted in their created worth which was reaffirmed in Christ. The text then says that 'he began to hate her', more keenly than he had desired her to begin with. After Tamar's refusal to leave, Amnon commands his servant to 'send this away' (the word 'woman' is added by translators for clarity). Tamar is left standing outside the door crying; she symbolically mourns her violation with ashes and tears the robe which is no longer appropriate clothing for her: after the rape, she is no longer one of the king's virgin daughters.

A number of important themes for understanding abuse emerge from this powerful and disturbing story. To begin with, abuse is linked to serious, even *shattering* harm.[18] It is clear that the damage done to Tamar is incalculable. It affects her present situation in immediate ways: what she can wear and where she can live. And it affects her future: what she can hope for. It affects her sense of self, her well-being, her dignity, at the deepest level: she is overwhelmed by consciousness of having suffered something 'vile' (verse 12), and becomes 'a desolate woman' (verse 20).

Second, the abuse is made possible by a relative imbalance of power. As a daughter of the king, Tamar herself would have been a powerful person, for instance in relation to her servants. Relative to Amnon, however, and indeed to David, she is in a position of weakness. She could not refuse to follow the king's orders, whether or not she had any misgivings about the assignment of visiting her sick half-brother. When he sends the servants away to leave them alone together, she cannot effectively protest. When he decides to use physical force to rape her, 'being stronger than she was' (verse 14), he prevails, despite her resistance.

Third, the imbalance of power is linked to the responsibility (and the consequent authority) entrusted to the abuser. Power is given to kings so that they may secure justice for those under their sovereignty, which includes protecting those who are most vulnerable from manifest injustice. Men are trusted to be alone with female family members, who would never otherwise be willingly left exposed to the risk of rape, because it is assumed that they will have a strong sense of care for their well-being and a respect for their dignity that will safely prevent them from behaving in such a way. Instead, however, the abuser, trusted to respond to those within their responsibility and therefore within the reach of their power as persons evoking care and respect, treats their victim as an object to be used and discarded. All human relationships involve trust, and, as such, the giving over of power by some to others. This takes place in many different ways, but wherever it happens the consequent dynamics of power provide scope for abusers to operate.

Finally, in order to misuse the power that comes from being trusted to behave with responsibility and therefore given authority, abusers must deceive others, and even themselves. The abuser lies to the victim to enable the abuse to happen; but, crucially, the abuser must also hide the truth from others. What the abuser wants threatens the position of responsibility through which he has the power to achieve it. Because the abuser has to retain the position of trusted responsibility, bound up with their exercise of power, in order to abuse, deception is a necessity. Moreover, deception of others is bound up with a certain masking of the truth from oneself: in order to carry on exercising their position of responsibility, the abuser may find it easier to hide the truth of what they have done even from themselves, at least some of the time. Hence Amnon's response after the abuse: 'Send this away'. Self-deceit can begin with the act of abuse itself: a study of clergy who had admitted to the sexual abuse of children found that in a number of cases they convinced themselves that the children concerned consented to what was done to them and could not therefore be considered as victims.[19] Unfortunately, some in wider society would affirm that distorted view.

The narrative of the rape of Tamar highlights four interrelated dimensions for understanding abuse: serious harm on the part of the victim; made possible by an imbalance of power in the particular situation obtaining between victim and perpetrator; linked to the perpetrator's position of trust; and abetted by deceit on the perpetrator's behalf, who uses the power that comes from this position to act in a way that contradicts the responsibility and trust associated with it. These four dimensions constitute a framework for understanding what is meant by 'abuse' that is neither too narrow to do justice to the variety of situations where it is relevant (see Introduction, pages 19–21) nor so open-ended that it is hard to identify its limits.

This framework is not intended to serve as a strict definition of abuse, or restrict the use of the term or displace other ways in which abuse may be characterized, such as failure to honour the image of God in another person. One or more of the four dimensions given above might be weak or absent in a particular case; others could doubtless be suggested in addition. The aim here is rather to offer an initial account of what is characteristic of the kind of actions that we refer to as 'abuse' – what makes them different from other kinds of harm and serious wrongdoing. It is an account that resists reducing the characterization of abuse to a single feature, or focusing solely on the experience of the person abused, the behaviour of the person abusing, or the nature of the relation between them. All of these are relevant for understanding abuse. This account also seeks to avoid the risk of circularity in drawing on the concept of abuse (or misuse) to explain what we mean by 'abuse'.

The Church of England's policy literature highlights the abuse of power as a principal dimension of abuse.[20] In doing so, it follows an important strand in both secular and theological writing about abuse.[21] The framework being proposed here does not take issue with this, but rather seeks to set out what the particular form of power that is being abused might be. Any harm done by one person to another involves an abuse of power at some level: by definition, human action deploys human powers, and therefore every wrong action against another person involves the misuse of human powers to that person's harm, since all power comes from God and is meant for good. We now turn our attention to this idea.

The concept of power has been much discussed by sociologists and philosophers in recent decades,[22] and the significant debate about power has received attention from theologians.[23] For Christians, the hermeneutic of suspicion about power in some of this literature, more or less identifying power with (oppressive) domination of others, cannot be the only lens for viewing it. God is 'almighty', and that is a reason for rejoicing, not cause for fear and suspicion. In God, all power is held by one who is also worthy of all our trust, and utterly faithful, carrying out what is promised and acting for justice. While there is no clear identification of divine action or intention in 2 Samuel 13—14, its literary context within 2 Samuel, and within the canon of Scripture as a whole, affirms that the purposes of the one God who is faithful and true are indeed at work in human affairs, and will finally prevail.

An understanding of abuse that is too narrow, or theologically unbalanced, may skew the church's approach to the challenges of safeguarding from abuse. For example, isolating the dimension of the imbalance of power may lead to the implication that the most effective form of safeguarding is simply to reduce all inequalities of power as far as possible. This depends on the assumption that power *as such* corrupts people, so that we can expect relatively powerful people to exploit their position at the expense of others. Thinking this way leads to the gloomy conclusion that the more powerful someone is, the less they should be trusted, and that the best way to organize things is to minimize power differentials between people.

Yet human life and human community depend on the responsible exercise of power by those entrusted with it. This is fundamental both to the care of the vulnerable (of all ages) beginning before birth, and to the nature of intimacy – a situation of mutual vulnerability. In the case of two adults, such entrusting of power may begin as a mutual and free exchange, while in the case of other relationships (parents and children), it is given by social and cultural norms, in turn reflecting biological realities. Yet even here, the distribution of power is not simply fixed or static, nor is the vulnerability all on one side. In their care for a growing child, parents face the challenge of remaining vulnerable within the relationship while at the same time providing security by maintaining appropriate boundaries. In an intimate relationship between adults, one who has used power to care and to protect may begin to use it instead to hurt and to humiliate, and indeed oscillate unpredictably between the two.

Church life, like family life, depends on relationships where power is not equally distributed, and trust needs to be invested in those who occupy positions of power. Trust from those with less power needs to be met by responsibility from those with more power and more authority. Trust depends on truthfulness: that people act in accordance with their promises. There is no regulatory system that can prevent deceit, although a strong culture of accountability and transparency (which the churches have not always fostered) will make it more difficult for deceit to be sustained and pass undetected. The churches have a clear obligation in this regard, but it remains the case that making judgements about trust is part of the risk of human life, of human community and of receiving care from others.

While the nature of interpersonal power is certainly significant, therefore, for understanding abuse, questions about trust and the betrayal of trust by deceit also remain pivotal. In the context of safeguarding practice, then, it is proposed here that by 'abuse' is meant serious harm of one person by another (as judged by the person harmed, or those in a position of oversight, or both), in the context of a relationship that is framed by the power of the one who inflicts the harm. It characteristically involves a less powerful person being subjected to harmful behaviours, words or attitudes by someone they should be able to rely on to act responsibly for their best interests, and who uses deceit in order to act in a way that directly contradicts the responsibilities of their power within the situation.

2. What is distinctive about abuse as a form of sin?

The sin of abuse can have far-reaching and highly destructive effects on the person who suffers it: effects which last for a long time and affect many relationships, including the human–divine relationship. Recovery from abuse can be long, complicated and difficult. Memories may surface in an unexpected and distressing manner, and the emotional response to what is recalled may differ over time. For the abuser, abuse distorts the will and corrupts the conscience. Moreover, abuse may be the occasion which draws into sin others who hold responsibility in the relevant institution and society for ensuring that justice is done and seen to be done. Those who become aware of abuse may fail to respond appropriately and so compound the sin, for example by denying or concealing the abuse, or by giving way to hatred and vengeance. This failure undermines the work of the justice which is achieved by the public, effective and visible work of the government, law and statutory authorities charged with prosecuting injustice without fear or favour. This 'temporal' justice is commissioned by God to do its work and is of immense value to society, especially to victims of abuse. Accordingly, it should be held in high esteem by the Church of England, and especially by those who hold responsibility within it.

Abuse is wrong. It transgresses the boundaries of mutual respect, and breaks agreements, understandings and conventions between fellow humans; it also fundamentally turns away from the purposes for which God created human relationships. It involves the utter perversion of the relationality which is at the heart of God's intent for human beings to live in God's image and to flourish together. Turning away from the good, and twisting relationships to purposes contrary to those for which they were created, causes damaging rifts that reach deep into the inner life of the abused person. The effects of abuse also extend far out into the fabric of interpersonal and institutional relationships in which it takes place. Such destructive effects can reverberate for decades, even beyond the lifetimes of those originally involved.

In Christian terms, abuse is a form of sin. That is the necessary theological condition for teaching about forgiveness to be relevant: forgiveness is needed because sin has happened, and sin is truly serious. It is needed because the wrong that has been done matters radically and profoundly; it is not something we could or should 'get over', or put to one side. In the light of the gospel, forgiveness is *always* relevant where sin has been committed: there is no situation of sin where God's power to bring forgiveness through the cross of Christ is simply inapplicable. Those who have to face the realities of abuse may find themselves starting to doubt this: the ramifications of evil are so deep and wide-ranging that it can seem impossible that forgiveness might extend to and embrace them all. Before asking how the church may seek to speak of forgiveness and reconciliation in the aftermath of abuse, we must therefore sketch out the characteristic shape that sin takes in this situation.

This section of the document begins by building on the framework
for understanding abuse set out in the previous section, based
on the four dimensions of abuse summarized on page 36. It continues
to explore the account of the rape of Tamar in 2 Samuel 13, using the
four categories of people involved in abuse that were suggested in
the Introduction (page 18): victim; perpetrator; those who hold
responsibility for prevention and response; and bystander.

As to the victim, the effect of Amnon's sin on Tamar herself is described
only briefly, though nonetheless powerfully. Phyllis Trible notes that the
verb used to describe her putting ash on her head in verse 19 is the
same one used of her taking dough to make bread in verse 8. Trible
writes that the 'action intent upon restoring life to her sick brother
becomes her own movement towards living death'.[24] Her grief is
described in the strongest terms in verse 20, which says that she
lived as a 'desolate' woman from that point on. The same Hebrew
word is used in Lamentations 1.16 and 3.11 to refer to Israel after
the Babylonian exile. She is lifeless, deserted, with no hope of a loving
husband or children. She is also unable to live in the palace after the
rape, perhaps due to the shame discussed above, and the trauma of
contact with Amnon, her abuser. The experience has shattered her
and taken away her home, her social identity and the future she had
hoped for.

The first and primary expression of the evil that is at work in abuse,
then, is in its impact on the person who suffers it. Such shattering harm
is not necessarily the result of a single, overwhelming blow. Abuse can
be chronic, and its force may come from actions repeated many times

over. The effects may be cumulative and slow to manifest, but they are likely to be far-reaching, and this is what the use of 'shattering' here is intended to convey. Early Christian writers, speaking in and to a Greco-Roman culture in which the sexual abuse of children by adults was part of accepted social behaviour, coined the word *paidophthoros* as a counter to the normal *paidoerastes* to express their opposition – the Greek word *phthora* meaning 'ruin' or 'destruction'. They wanted to say that such treatment is not loving, but corrupting and profoundly destructive.[25]

It needs to be constantly kept in mind that making reliable generalizations about abuse is not straightforward. The social-scientific research literature on abuse highlights the difficulty of establishing reliable data in this field, the striking diversity of human behaviour that is being studied and the contested nature of all explanatory descriptions.[26] Moreover, it is vital to listen to the voices of those who have suffered abuse in order to begin to understand their experience. Alistair McFadyen comments that 'The pathological effects of childhood sexual abuse can be, and often are, severe, deep-seated and long-lasting. They are also highly particular. What the reality of abuse actually is for any individual child or adult survivor – how it is experienced, the nature and extent of its effects – relates to a complex interaction of factors, which will be unique in every case. Because the experience of being abused and of surviving is idiosyncratic, it is not possible to give a unitary account that will hold true for all survivors.'[27]

As noted above, the biblical narrator in 2 Samuel 13 makes clear
the depth of the damage done by the abuse without dwelling on
it at any great length. There is, indeed, a place for a proper reticence
here. In order to understand how abuse affects people, we need to be
willing to listen to people who have been abused and attend to their
stories.[28] Where we cannot hear their voices, we should be wary of
imagining that we can construct narratives of response for ourselves.
Arising from such attention, however, there will also be a legitimate
concern to identify common patterns and themes as part of the work
of understanding.

One such theme is that of 'brokenness', with reference to a wide range
of personal, relational and social effects. As in the case of Tamar, these
may include rejection imposed by others, or isolation sought by the
person abused because of an overwhelming feeling of shame, leading
to a deep sense of desolation. All this may also become bound up with
feelings of guilt, that somehow the one abused is responsible for the
abuse, or deserved it because of their failures and lack of worth (as in
the fictional situation of 'Darren' at the end of section 5 below). Working
through such feelings and the associated perception that the abuse
was 'my fault' can be a significant dimension of pastoral ministry with
survivors, and one that has specific relevance for how the church speaks
to them about forgiveness. Letting go of the perception of fault may
mean fully facing the extent of helplessness and victimhood, while at
the same time finding some sense of agency rather than total passivity.
This is vital and difficult work, and specialist training is crucial.

A number of studies have explored the effects of abuse on a person's selfhood, with the concept of *trauma* seen by many as very helpful.[29] Memories can lie buried for many years, before people become deeply disturbed by what they then become able to recall in later life.[30] As with other kinds of trauma, precise effects vary from person to person and from day to day for the same person and include depression, anxiety, dissociation and anger.

Abuse can trigger a profound dislocation of normal patterns of memory, emotion and behaviour. What language can express the reality of the loss that may ensue? One survivor of trauma speaks of a kind of *death*, such that she struggled to recognize herself as the same person she had been before the event of abuse, citing many others from different contexts who have experienced something analogous after suffering shattering harm.[31] In a more overtly theological vein, Susan Shooter writes about the 'annihilation of the soul', using a metaphor from medieval mysticism to articulate the depth of the evil done through abuse.[32]

It was noted in the previous section that shattering harm in abuse is bound up with the abuse of power and the betrayal of trust. For the abused person, this may then obstruct the positive giving of trust to others that is integral to intimacy, love and the experience of acceptance: fundamental goods of human existence. The initial 'shattering' may spread out to put fractures in relations with those perceived to be somehow associated with the abuser, for instance other family members, or those linked to the institution within which the abuse occurred. It may become radically pervasive, touching all the relationships that the abused person has, insofar as those relationships imply an invitation to trust another person with power and have confidence in their truthfulness and care. That can include the relationship with God, as one who is all-powerful, and in whom we are asked to put our trust. How the experience of abuse affects the practice of faith, the life of prayer and the development of spirituality for the person abused is a vital subject for further reflection within the churches.[33]

The previous section (page 35) touched on the effects of Amnon's sin on himself, the perpetrator. The sin involves a denial of Tamar's humanity, perpetuated by the refusal to acknowledge what he has done and a determination to carry on as though nothing has changed. Denial and deceit are woven together, in such a way as to hollow out his conscience and undermine the capacity to act responsibly and consistently. The destructive effects of abuse on the abuser themselves are also considered in the companion document to this one, *The Gospel, Sexual Abuse and the Church: A Theological Resource for the Local Church*.

Talk about 'the perpetrator' may obscure the reality that a number of people have collaborated in order for abuse to happen. In the narrative of 2 Samuel 13, for instance, a key role is played by Amnon's friend, Jonadab: he is the one who tells Amnon, 'son of the king', that he should not accept the frustration of his desires, and he is the 'very crafty man' who devises the successful plan to trap Tamar in Amnon's bedroom (2 Samuel 13.3–5). He may not be an abuser as such, but for his own reasons he has assisted in abuse being committed. What of his sin? In our own time, globalization and electronic communication multiply the potential agents of abuse, who, like Jonadab, incite those who might otherwise restrain themselves from putting thought into action, and use their intelligence and skill to create opportunities for abuse and to trap its victims. Human trafficking, often with a dimension of prostitution, and internet pornography are promoted on an industrial scale by international organized crime, feeding off the desperation engendered by poverty and forced migration.

Those who have been victims of abuse of this kind – who might be our neighbours or colleagues at work – may struggle to give a name and a face to those responsible for the crimes they have suffered, both because there are so many people involved and because they may only have actually met a few of them (and not perhaps those who carry the most guilt). The dynamics of sin become more complex in such a dispersed situation, but they are no less real. Indeed, the illusion they foster, of absence of guilt for any particular individual within the system, is a part of how sin is at work.

In the second half of 2 Samuel 13, the focus moves away from Tamar and Amnon to David and Absalom. Indeed, the overarching focus of the narrative is on the failures of David as the person with responsibility for preventing and responding to this kind of wrongdoing. David is angry (verse 21): he does not regard Amnon's behaviour as a minor offence that can be easily overlooked. Yet he will not do anything about it. He will not take any kind of action against Amnon that would either publicly make clear that Amnon has committed a grave wrong, or limit his ability to repeat it in another context. David's refusal to exercise his authority as father and king to address what has happened contributes to the way that the effects of sin spread and grow in this situation.

The twin stories of Bathsheba and Tamar in 2 Samuel 11–13 must be seen in the context of the long-running Old Testament debate over the role of kings. Supporters of kingship see establishing justice and protection as the basis of royal rule. For example, the author of Judges brackets another horrific account of abuse with reference to a future monarchy in which it would not happen (Judges 19.1, 21.25). David repeatedly fails to uphold what is just and instead, through his abusive actions, denies the equal worth of Bathsheba, Uriah and Tamar. This failure to ensure the proper exercise of 'temporal' justice is therefore a critical blow to his authority as king. David is angry in verse 21, but that anger does not lead to justice for Tamar. He holds responsibility for maintaining justice, but he does not seek justice, and therefore he himself is judged. The sin of abuse meshes with the sins of those who hold such responsibility but do not use it rightly, first finding a foothold because of those sins and then extending them by drawing those with that responsibility into deepening collusion through their failure to act.

Beyond those who hold specific responsibility for preventing and responding to abuse, there is the broader category of those who are 'bystanders' – those who become aware of it and are affected by that awareness in various ways. In 2 Samuel 13, it is clear that most of the bystanders as thus defined carry on without comment. They know, but they put that knowledge to one side and continue to treat Amnon as they had previously. This is not, sadly, surprising. Human aversion to dwelling on horror and trauma is not simply perverse.[34] To look and listen is costly. In the case of abuse, it is difficult to listen with sustained attention to the witness of the victim without needing to challenge the continuing position and power of the perpetrator and the lies that sustain them. That may be dangerous, and the price may be high.

The narrative, however, focuses on one bystander in particular who does listen and who is determined to act: Absalom. David has the authority to take action, but does nothing. Absalom, on the other hand, does not have the authority but cannot abide the vacuum created by his father. So he will take action of his own: not justice, but murder. He is consumed by the need to punish the abuser, a need that can only be quenched by his death. Absalom cannot envisage the restoration of his relationship with Amnon, nor suffer Amnon to continue to live in a shared community or society with him. Absalom may be motivated at some level by concern for justice, but the perversion of that concern by hatred leads him to commit injustice of his own, which further contributes to the spread of the evil unleashed by Amnon's act of abuse. First, he takes the law into his own hands, and then he ultimately attempts to oust David as king. Absalom's violence in ordering the murder of Amnon at a family gathering is intended as revenge for the rape of his sister, and is a further violation of the claims of justice inherent in humanity's created worth and a further distortion of the work of temporal justice. Far from bringing some kind of resolution, it only leads to further acts of abuse, such as an early example of rape as a weapon of war, as Absalom publicly rapes David's concubines in 2 Samuel 16.20–23 – the women being seen as David's possessions, therefore making the rape an act against his property.

To become a bystander to abuse – someone who knows something about what has happened but does not have the authority or courage to address the wrong that has been done – is to enter a difficult place. For reasons that have been noted, it is not easy to give space to someone who has been abused to tell their story, or even simply to acknowledge the full scale of what has happened to them. Bystanders may feel pulled between the apparently contradictory though ultimately related reactions of denial and demonization. Denial carries on as if nothing has happened, perpetuating the deceit that is one of the dimensions of abuse and contributing to the failure to seek justice on which abuse depends. Demonization on the other hand gives free rein to hate and hurt the offender, and thereby multiply sins. Denial will not contemplate the reality of what has happened to the abused person, while demonizing perpetrators as 'evil' and as 'monsters' who must be excluded from the human community effaces their humanity in turn. If many bystanders to abuse in the churches in the past have been guilty of collusion with denial, it would be regrettable if reaction to this pushed them instead towards the demonization that holds such evident attraction in our contemporary culture.

The sin of abuse has far-reaching effects for those who are its victims, including those who become its survivors (for not all survive). It will be crucial to have these in mind when attention turns in section 5 to the question: 'How should the church speak of forgiving to those who have experienced abuse?' Abuse has very different but still far-reaching effects on those who commit it, and it is vital to have some grasp of this in order to answer the fourth question addressed by this document: 'How should the church speak of being forgiven to those who have committed abuse?' Before that, however, it is important to acknowledge that churches, and church leaders in particular, may also share something of David's place in the Tamar narrative: those who have a part in the responsibility for preventing and responding to abuse, and who fail to exercise their responsibility well.

PART II

Responding to Abuse

3. Is there a place for repentance by churches where they have shared in some way in the sin of abuse?

The church as the body of Christ has sometimes failed to respond with justice and compassion for the abused when its members have committed sins of abuse. It needs to acknowledge its part in compounding those sins and change its ways. It also needs to work out its relationship with those who have suffered on account of the naivety, negligence and complicity that have let the church become an arena of abuse. Apology may well be required but in a Christian context cannot be separated from the call to repentance. Like all repentance, this cannot be achieved merely by words or gestures, but needs to be a thoroughgoing change of attitude, thinking and behaviour. The concept of ecclesial repentance is significant here and should be carefully considered by the Church of England. One critical question that needs to be faced is how far weak or misleading doctrine has contributed to the church's failings in preventing and responding to abuse. A false opposition between forgiveness and justice would be one example of this.

One dimension of the churches' involvement with abuse is that they share responsibility with other institutions within society, including the relevant statutory agencies, for preventing and responding to abuse. Churches, including the Church of England, have sometimes failed in the duties that follow from this responsibility, including the cooperation that it requires with others. Where people have used their positions of authority and associated trust in the life of the church to commit abuse, questions ought to be asked: both about what could have been done to prevent this from having happened, and about what should be done now to prevent it from recurring, by the actions of the original perpetrator or of others in parallel contexts. Specific people hold the responsibility in each case for asking those questions, pursuing them and taking action in light of the answers to them. Failures to act properly are still coming to light, and it is likely that they will continue to do so, not least as the government's inquiry into historic cases of child abuse unfolds. How should churches respond? How should they acknowledge their failures?

Where it is evident that there have been failures to act in accordance with what is recognized as due procedure by particular individuals or bodies with responsibility, an unambiguous apology is needed.[35] There are some challenges here: we live in a society where apologies are constantly demanded, and indeed offered with some frequency, yet the volatile exchanges of this currency do not always serve to hold up its value. Official statements of apology may leave issues of responsibility for what happened and accountability for addressing it ambiguous. But what is an apology worth if it does not convey a clear apprehension of responsibility and accountability, together with evidence of a change of practice aimed at avoiding repetition of the offence? It is estimated that in 2002 alone, the Roman Catholic Church in the USA issued over twenty statements of formal apology for failings with regard to sexual abuse by its officers and representatives. Yet there was 'widespread perception ... that these apologies were inadequate'.[36] That perception persisted in public responses to high-profile papal apologies in 2008 (again in the USA) and 2010 (in Ireland).

Whatever pressures there may be for speed, the need remains for attentive listening to those who have suffered because of churches' mistakes. An apology is primarily for them and addressed to them. Addressing those who have suffered from the churches' mistakes means seeking to understand their concerns and their perspectives, in a way that they can receive and, in turn, respond to. This may not be an easy process. When those who have been abused begin to organize their thoughts and feelings and to speak to the churches, there is great anger. This anger must be heard and felt – not only as the indignation of the ill-treated, or even the rage of the wounded, but as a prophetic voice which is saying to the church that it has not yet fully understood the nature or extent of the scandal for which it bears responsibility. In other words, this cry is not a cry for help, or for healing, or even for apology. It is a prophetic cry for repentance by the churches.

There is indeed a need for repentance as well as apology. Failures to protect the weak from the strong in this matter are not simply a breach of procedure that may lead to professional or legal sanction, but are instances of sin – as suggested in the previous section, sin that all too commonly both enables and is occasioned by the sin of abuse itself. Without equating clergy or other church officers with the monarchs and other authorities of ancient Israel, the expectations of those entrusted with leadership among the people of God in the Old Testament are clear: as with David in 2 Samuel, they are to uphold the requirements of justice, including the proper exercise of 'temporal justice' as described in the Introduction (page 26). God's people are under God's judgement when they consistently refuse to do this.

Ezekiel 34 is a particularly vivid denunciation of the sins of those entrusted with responsibilities of leadership for God's people. The shepherds have devoured the sheep (verses 3, 10) and have also neglected to feed and care for them. As Keith Carley points out, 'while the shepherds exploited their rights to the full, they utterly neglected their duties'.[37] The shepherds are not 'outsiders' who have no business being with the sheep, but they have abused their rightful position. Such abuse is harder to see or to deal with than external oppression, which is why it is the primary focus of the oracle. The shepherds have neglected the weakest of the flock in particular, such as those who are injured or sick (verse 4). As a result, the flock is scattered (verse 5). The shepherds are not only a threat to the flock themselves, but their complacency has left the sheep open to attack. The rulers, then, have not only abused the people themselves but have also left those in their care vulnerable to abuse by others. By contrast, the Davidic shepherd in verses 23–25 foreshadows Christ, the Son of David, who acts as God's representative and loves the weak. The passage makes it clear that the 'leadership of God's covenant people carries with it obligations of selfless service'.[38]

This chapter from Ezekiel was not a comfortable passage of prophecy to hear in the sixth century BC, and it is not a comfortable passage to hear today either. It is a matter of public record that when cases of serious abuse have come to their attention, churches have not always acted in a way that expressed a grasp of the depth of the sin involved, and in particular the extent of the harm done to the victims of abuse. Churches, including the Church of England, have focused instead on the risk of damage to themselves: damage to their ministry through abuse by church members and officers becoming known, and damage to the spiritual, moral and psychological health of clergy abusers in particular. Effort was consequently given to the management of reputational, financial and legal risk, and on the intended rehabilitation of clerical offenders through internal discipline and attempted treatment. The shepherds took good care of themselves, when their primary concern should have been for the sheep, above all those who were 'weak' and 'injured', and vulnerable to being made 'food for wild animals' (verses 4–6).

Failures by churches with regard to their responsibilities for preventing and responding to abuse require both public apology and repentance that follows from reflection on the scale of the sins that have been committed, not just by the abuser but by those holding these responsibilities. Who is it, however, who is called to repent? Beyond the particular individuals who can be identified as having made wrong decisions at specific points, is this a matter for anyone else? Is it a matter for the particular church as a body, as part of the body of Christ? And what if they are unwilling to apologize and repent, or unable to because they have died? We understand apologies given on behalf of another – but can someone repent on another person's behalf?

Debates around collective guilt that emerged in the aftermath of the Second World War have continued to attract critical attention ever since.[39] If there can be collective responsibility for wrongdoing, does this require a collective apology? What would such an apology mean in practice? Can institutions ask for forgiveness – and if so, from whom?[40] A significant academic literature has developed that reflects on the various questions here, drawing on philosophy, politics and sociology.[41] Intersecting with this phenomenon is the specifically theological issue of ecclesial repentance, prompted not least by parallel concerns about complicity in the crimes of the Second World War.[42] Repentance in the Scriptures is often a corporate rather than a purely individual act. Cities repent (cf. Matthew 11.20, 12.45, Luke 10.31–3, 11.32, 13.3–5), and the calls to repent issued by John the Baptist and Jesus of Nazareth, echoing the Old Testament prophets, are primarily for the repentance of the whole people, not just selected individuals. Yet what can it mean for the church, which continues that call of sinners to repentance, to repent of its own actions? How can the one, holy, catholic and apostolic church acknowledge that it has failed to be holy, and thereby failed to be the church? If by sin it has failed to *be* the church, how can it repent *as* the church?

Over the past hundred years, churches have made numerous public statements that express contrition for implication in sin that is not simply about the misconduct of individual members, nor the failures of particular communities or parts of the institution, but is somehow the shared responsibility of all. It is perhaps worth noting that the 'Appeal to all Christian People' of the 1920 Lambeth Conference has some claim to being the earliest major example of this, and repentance for contribution to the sins of division continued to be a significant feature of ecumenical engagement for much of the twentieth century. Churches have issued statements of apology or repentance (the terminology tends to be fluid) in relation to the legacy of colonialism, war and violence, injustice and maltreatment of the environment.[43] A debate at General Synod in 2006 regarding the Church of England's response to the commemoration of the abolition of the slave trade included significant exchanges about whether this should include a formal apology for its own complicity in it.[44] The motion that was finally approved included reference to this, and the public apology subsequently made by the Archbishop of Canterbury received widespread and generally positive publicity in the mainstream media.

Ecclesial repentance raises some substantial theological issues. Most obviously, it touches on long-standing discussions about the relationship between the holiness that is one of the creedal marks of the church and the reality of continuing sin in the life of the church.[45] In the context of Roman Catholic thought in particular, there is a powerful line of argument to the effect that the church, as such, cannot sin, although of course the church is made up of sinful men and women, and therefore the church (as opposed to its individual members) cannot repent either.[46] Protestant ecclesiology with its historical emphasis on *ecclesia semper reformanda* ('the church is always to be reformed') tends to be critical of this approach; Luther once said, 'There is no greater sinner than the church.'[47] Are we prepared to say that the church, made holy by Christ and called to share the good news with the world, is deeply marked by sin and needs *to receive* what it mediates to others – and who will be *its* mediator? Or are we inclined in the end to displace that guilt onto something other than the church in which we believe according to the creed, onto a 'merely' human institution? To remain committed to the difficult notion of ecclesial repentance is to grapple with the paradox that the church can sometimes fail to be what it is – and yet it remains one reality, not two.

Ecclesial repentance also raises questions of representation: who speaks the words of repentance, on whose behalf, and what are the conditions for a representative figure speaking in this way? It is part of the teaching of the Church of England that clergy represent the church in their ministry: ordination designates a person as trusted with responsibility to speak publicly before God for the whole church, those in that place and those associated with them in the body of Christ. In an Anglican context, therefore, it is not a strange thing for an archbishop to acknowledge failings on the part of the national church, a bishop on behalf of their diocese, or a priest on the part of their parish, and in doing so to be heard as saying something that also relates to the life of the church universal, grappling with the paradox of its sinfulness and sanctity.

In such a situation, it may also be right for the bishop or priest to express the repentance of that part of the church they are representing. The power of an act of ecclesial repentance of this kind depends crucially on clarity that the person who speaks representatively is truly speaking *with* the church, as well as truly attending to those who have been wronged and to whom the church would now speak. That means that others in the church also need to be given time to reflect on what has happened, what has gone wrong and the distribution of responsibility for it, and the opportunity to associate themselves with the formal act of repentance, perhaps through appropriate symbols and ritual expression as well as commitment to concrete action to put right wrong that was done.

To go back to an example mentioned earlier, part of the power of the apology for involvement with slavery in 2006 was that it followed a motion at General Synod, and there was therefore a formal expression of the fact that when the Archbishop made a public statement, he uttered words that were 'meant' by the Church of England as a whole and was not just making some kind of praiseworthy gesture as an individual Christian leader. At the same time, the Archbishop had made it clear in his contribution to the debate that such an apology as an act of the church held together the living and the dead: 'The body of Christ is not just a body that exists at any one time; it exists across history and we therefore share the shame and sinfulness of our predecessors and part of what we can do, with them and for them in the Body of Christ, is prayerful acknowledgement of the failure that is part of us not just of some distant "them".'

Repentance, whether individual or corporate, requires a willingness to commit to action that seeks to make good the wrong that has been done, as well as the clear and unequivocal naming of the wrong that has been committed. There is a long tradition of reflection about this in relation to the ministry of absolution, which will be considered further in the next section. Of course, no action can make up for the damage that has been done by the evil of abuse. Clear commitment to action that can bring change from the past is, however, an integral element of the church's acknowledgement of its share in that sin. This is classically a part of what reconciliation or penance requires. Repentance for the Christian means a promise to walk in newness of life. Statements of corporate apology that do not unambiguously convey both the acknowledgement of collective failings and the commitment to put them right make little sense, in secular or theological terms.

Finally, ecclesial repentance generally involves the acknowledgement that while theology can enable sin to be identified and rooted out it can also play a part in enabling sin to take root. There are various places one might look for wrong teaching in the context of responding to abuse, with some of its dimensions identified elsewhere in this document and the companion piece from the Faith and Order Commission. Some would want to go beyond the areas addressed directly here and argue that church doctrine and liturgy remain permeated, for instance, by patriarchal and feudal modes of thinking that are instrumental in setting up and sustaining distorted relationships within the life of the church. With respect to justice, how doctrine concerning Christ's atoning work is taught will also be important in ensuring that the righteousness of God which saves is presented as the basis for pursuing temporal justice in cases of abuse rather than suggesting that the church's internal processes of discipline, forgiveness and repentance make the pursuit of such justice unnecessary. Such far-reaching critiques, arising from reflection on the experience of survivors, deserve careful attention.

One clear example of problematic theology in this context is the separation of justice from the gospel of salvation. Scripture is clear that God's 'eschatological' justice or 'righteousness' (page 27 above) is not to be opposed to God's salvation: a passage such as Isaiah 59 is wholly based on the assumption that God's righteousness saves those who suffer injustice, and God's salvation establishes justice on the earth. God is 'appalled' when there is no one to stand for justice and wrongdoing continues unchecked (Isaiah 59.16). As we read elsewhere in Isaiah, 'There is no other God besides me, a righteous God and a Saviour' (45.21). Persistent failure in the exercise of 'temporal' justice incurs God's judgement. Nor is this a perspective that is somehow set aside by the gospel of Jesus Christ, who summons us to seek first God's kingdom and its righteousness (Matthew 6.33). In Christ, and him crucified, 'every one of God's promises is a "Yes"' (2 Corinthians 1.20), including God's promise of justice restored. The church that proclaims the good news of transforming forgiveness also witnesses to the seriousness of sin through its commitment to temporal justice, its upholding of the justice inherent in created order and reaffirmed in Christ and its practice of the virtue of justice. This will be explored further in the following section.

Fictional Case Study: St Matthew's

St Matthew's is a residential care home that began life as a 'mission to the aged' from St Matthew's parish church in the 1880s. It has retained strong Anglican associations ever since, with the incumbent and churchwardens being on the Board of Trustees. A year ago a new Chief Executive was appointed who rapidly became concerned about the standards of care and the attitudes of staff. He found complaints and concerns of neglect and physical harm to residents which had not been addressed by the previous manager. The new Chief Executive referred these complaints to the police for criminal investigation, and asked the local authority to undertake an inspection. The outcome of police investigations and the local authority inspection, which received wide local publicity, revealed that for a period of at least ten years standards of care had been low, the mortality rate for the home was exceptionally high and that the level of neglect amounted to systemic abuse, and included allegations of cruelty.

The incumbent of St Matthew's is a much loved pastor whose retirement is approaching. He is well known for not having a good grasp on administration, and for being unable to deal with conflict. He avoids discussion with the Chief Executive, and has not been able to address the 'fall out' of this report, or his own role in the failings of the home, with his congregation.

The Archdeacon and the Diocesan Safeguarding Adviser are concerned about the impact on the church and parish of the reports of the failings of the home. In addition to the incumbent and the churchwardens being members of the Board, a number of members of the congregation visit residents voluntarily. Some present and past members of the congregation or their family members are or have been residents in the home themselves.

General considerations in responding

The response to this case must pay heed to the Safeguarding policies and procedures of the home. Because of the strong parish links, these would need to link to Church of England Practice Guidance 'Responding to Serious Safeguarding Situations', and a diocesan/parish core group should have been set up to manage the process when complaints first arose.

The core group would address processes for a wide range of issues, including:

- Referral to statutory agencies (police and social services), following their lead and implementing their advice.
- Providing support to all those involved, including residents and their families, affected members of the congregation, staff, the incumbent, and the churchwardens.
- Following legal procedures and informing insurers.
- Managing communication and reputational damage.
- Managing the impact on the congregation, both immediate and long term. This in particular involves responding to the spiritual and emotional needs of individuals affected, and to the whole congregation.

Possible responses which may be considered:

- The archdeacon or bishop might support the incumbent by giving clear information in person to parishioners following the report, and offering immediate and ongoing support to anyone affected (e.g. a Listener available when the information is given, and an advertised phone number).
- A bridge-building/reconciliation process might be instituted for a time following the report, facilitated by an external agency such as Bridge Builders, in order to rebuild trust, enable hurt, shame and sadness to be expressed, and creating the conditions for a corporate acknowledgement of harm done.

Questions about forgiveness and reconciliation

In the short term, how might the sadness, regret and anger felt within the congregation and wider community be acknowledged and expressed, without passing judgement on the question of who is responsible for failures? How can the incumbent and Archdeacon enable conversations that both acknowledge what has happened and seek to place it in the light of the gospel? What could be a suitable scripture passage to preach from, and what could be some key messages? What kind of opportunities to address the situation in personal prayer and public worship might be appropriate?

At some point, for personal, spiritual and professional reasons, the incumbent will have to face his own role in the failings of the home.

If these are serious, should he apologize, and if so to whom? Would early retirement followed by an apology from the Archdeacon for the failings of others be preferable? If he wishes to continue in post, what may be needed to rebuild trust with the congregation and wider community, potentially while there is a disciplinary case hanging over him? It has been argued in this section that any kind of apology in the aftermath of abuse needs to (a) identify clearly the nature of the mistake or failure that has occurred, (b) state what will be done to address the situation and avoid recurrence and (c) be informed by careful listening to those affected by the abuse, including survivors. What might that mean in this particular context?

Formulating 'a corporate acknowledgement of harm done' is likely to take considerable time – not least because it will require potentially painful acknowledgement of different levels of failure by individuals and bodies representing the church. As just noted, acknowledging the harm done requires understanding it, and understanding it means listening to those who have suffered and those whose lives have been affected by the situation. This is going to involve spending time hearing what some very hurt and angry people have to say. Moreover, the example of the Archbishop of Canterbury's apology over slavery underlines that where one person wishes to speak on behalf of others in the church, then where possible those others should be given the opportunity to affirm their identification with what is being said.

Bound up with that challenging task will be questions about whether responsibility for what went wrong ultimately rests only on a number of particular individuals (for instance, the perpetrators themselves and the members of the governing body who failed in their legal responsibilities) or whether it also extends more widely to the local church community, or even to those in oversight at diocesan level. Was there a tacit agreement to look the other way, for instance? Was there a willingness to wave aside normal requirements of good governance on the grounds that we are all Christians and can trust one another? Was there an unwillingness to challenge the vicar's judgement (and if so, why)? Was there a reluctance to engage with others who should have been consulted, e.g. the Diocesan Safeguarding Adviser and the relevant statutory agencies? If the answer to any of these questions is yes, then it could be worth exploring whether problematic theology played a part in the failings. If so, that needs to be stated clearly, and wrong doctrine clearly rejected.

Finally, when all are agreed that the time for such corporate acknowledgement of harm is right, how should it be communicated, and by whom? How might the congregation recognize their possible corporate failings in a public way? How helpful are the Church of England's liturgical resources here (e.g. *Common Worship: Initiation Services*, pp. 228–63)? How might the generic public language of acknowledgement and apology be related to the church's distinctive language of sin, forgiveness and salvation in formal communication?

4. How should the church speak of being forgiven to those who have committed abuse?

God's offer of forgiveness through the cross of Christ is for all; none has the slightest claim or entitlement to it in light of their merits, and for each it opens up the way to transformation beyond any imagining. That is the good news, and it is the joyful duty of the church to proclaim it. Turning to God to receive forgiveness also means turning away from the wrong we have done, and recognizing it as sin that separates us from God and one another and binds us to death. Responding to God's offer of salvation therefore involves repentance as well as boundless thankfulness. In the case of those who have committed abuse, part of such repentance will be a willingness to face the consequences, including legal consequences, of acknowledging the sin that has been committed. This has implications for the ministry of absolution within the church. Moreover, the nature of abuse (and not least the way it may habituate the abuser to self-deceit) can make it difficult for repentance to take root. Evidence of repentance cannot mean that no constraints should be placed on a person's access to situations where re-offending would be possible.

According to a Church of England report, it would appear that 'a higher proportion of convicted offenders against children may be found in church congregations than in the population generally'.[48] Recent studies suggest that at least 25% of offenders against children and vulnerable people attend churches.[49] That may reflect the way that churches continue to be seen as a 'soft touch' by those who continue to seek opportunities to abuse others. Yet it also indicates both the opportunity and the responsibility that churches have to speak about forgiveness to abusers, whether convicted, accused or unidentified to the church community and wider society. Indeed, it is a reminder that whenever forgiveness is the subject of preaching and teaching, there is a reasonable possibility that abusers may be among those listening.

The Gospels record the declaration of God's forgiveness as a distinctive, and at times shocking, feature of Jesus' ministry (e.g. Mark 2.5–7). Jesus seeks out the most notorious of sinners and does not demand their repentance before he will keep company with them, although his presence elicits it (Luke 19.1–9). In the parable of the two sons, the motivations of the younger son for returning to the family home appear mixed at best, yet the sight of his son is sufficient to move the father to run towards him, ready to give the embrace of welcome, beyond all the son's expectations and before he can even begin to speak any words of contrition (Luke 11.11–24). God's word of forgiveness, in its scandalous generosity, is transformative and creative, establishing a new situation and calling those who are dead in sin to abundant life. It is a gift beyond anything we could ask or imagine, which includes the call to turn away from all that holds us captive by the power of sin and walk in newness of life, and the grace to hear and respond to it. There is no turning to God to receive forgiveness without the opening of the heart to the way of repentance.

The apostles could offer that same divine forgiveness to the crowds at Pentecost because of what God had done through Christ. When the crowds asked how they should respond to his message, Peter replies, 'Repent and be baptized every one of you in the name of Jesus Christ so that your sins will be forgiven; and you will receive the gift of the Holy Spirit' (Acts 2.38). To receive the gift there needs to be a beginning of the journey of repentance, a re-orientation of the person to God's kingdom and God's justice. The interweaving of forgiveness and repentance in their preaching might be compared to the way these are connected in the accounts of the ministry of John the Baptist (e.g. Mark 1.4, Luke 1.77; Matthew 3.1–12, Luke 3.1–22). Later Christian tradition emphasizes that repentance is itself the work of grace: it is by the gift of God that our hearts are made ready to receive 'redemption through his blood, the forgiveness of our trespasses, according to the riches of his grace' (Ephesians 1.7).

Forgiveness stands at the beginning of life in Christ yet Christians will not cease to find themselves in need of it. There is some indication that this troubled early believers, whose profound appreciation of what had happened in baptism appeared to be contradicted by the reality of continuing sinfulness (perhaps the situation referred to in Hebrews 10.26–31). This may also be at least part of the context for passages which comment on what we might call church discipline, such as Matthew 18.15–20, 2 Corinthians 2.5–11 and 1 Timothy 5.20.

In 1 Corinthians 5.1–5, Paul is responding to a serious case of sexual sin within the Corinthian congregation, and with the complacency of the church that allowed the offence to take place, which Anthony Thiselton refers to as 'the corporate sin of the community'.[50] The church is seen as a soft touch, tolerating behaviour that would merit condemnation in the world beyond it, despite claiming to be holy and separate. The sin of one member of the community and the complacency of the community as a whole are closely linked. Paul's call for mourning recognizes this connection, as he asks in verse 2: 'Should you not rather have mourned, so that he who has done this would have been removed from among you?' Corporate repentance and mourning is therefore intended to make individual complacency and sin intolerable.

Paul instructs the congregation to 'hand this man over to Satan'. Although some commentators have interpreted these words as an irrevocable anathema, salvation is clearly intended in verse 5, which expresses the hope that the offender's spirit will be saved on the Day of the Lord. It could be argued that the continuing offer of God's forgiveness is implicit in that hope.

The reference to the destruction of the flesh indicates that such an offer is not made lightly. Thiselton argues that 'flesh' here is not simply a reference to the physical body, but in line with Paul's use of the word elsewhere it means that the offender's pride and desire to sin are to be challenged through church discipline, bringing him to repentance and salvation.[51] While holding out the hope of forgiveness, such discipline does not minimize the seriousness of sin, demanding a repentance analogous to physical death.[52]

Sin, in the New Testament, is not simply something that sinners do but something that shapes their being so as to 'undo' it, reducing life in the body to 'flesh' turned in upon itself, which will ultimately consume itself. Release from sin through divine forgiveness is therefore ultimately inseparable from resurrection. God's forgiveness is not so much about waiving the consequences of sin as creating in limitless love and power new life beyond those consequences, in all their apparent finality.

A passage from the Doctrine Commission's report *The Mystery of Salvation* is worth citing at this point. It states that 'Sin is constituted by all the wrong deeds and thoughts which make us fail to hit the mark of the kind of people God intended us to be, all the badness in us that alienates us from his goodness and holiness. To suggest that at one fell swoop all that disappeared would be to reduce our faith to an implausible fairytale. Rather, what happens is that God assures us of a new status as we throw ourselves on his mercy, upon that offer of forgiveness from the cross. ... The result is not only a new status vis-à-vis God as accepted and forgiven in Christ but also a new status in respect of our relationships with fellow human beings. ... But that this much can be instantaneous should not be allowed to conceal from us the more gradual character of much else.'[53]

Biblical teaching on how God's forgiveness is received has also informed two thousand years of church tradition, including the practice of what in current documents the Church of England refers to as the 'ministry of absolution', known in modern Roman Catholic terminology as the 'sacrament of reconciliation' and in popular usage as 'confession'. To avoid confusion, the Church of England term is used in what follows.

There is a complex history here, and a controversial one within the Church of England itself.[54]

One of the recurrent issues within that history has been the relative emphasis placed on three interlinking relationships: between the sinner and God, the sinner and the church, and the sinner and the person sinned against. It is important to underline that the primary focus of the New Testament and of subsequent Christian teaching is on forgiveness as a divine–human interaction: humans repent and God forgives. It is an interaction that cannot, however, be separated from changes to the interaction between human beings, as it opens up new horizons for repentance and renewal there also, including the life of the church as a community of repentant and forgiven sinners. Still, in a contemporary context where the weight can sometimes seem to fall exclusively on forgiveness as a private transaction on the one hand between human individuals, or on the other between the soul and its God, the inseparability of these three relationships so far as Christian theology is concerned needs to be constantly borne in mind.

Receiving God's forgiveness cannot be divorced from repentance that is ready to seek restoration of relationships at the level of human community. This repentance can be demonstrated through 'restorative action' with regard both to those who have been wronged (cf. Zacchaeus in Luke 19) and also to those with whom the sinner shares a common life of holiness in Christ, which has been wounded by their actions (so 1 Corinthians 5.1–5). Such action belongs within John the Baptist's call for his hearers to 'bear fruit in keeping with repentance' (Matthew 3.8 and parallels). There will always be limits on what kind of action is possible here, but willingness to do what is possible is a mark of the repentance that leads to life.

Holding the three relationships together, however, becomes difficult once the churches move into the era of Christendom, because of overlapping social and ecclesial identities. In the church of the early centuries, those who had committed grave sins were publicly identified, excluded from the Eucharist and only formally re-admitted to eucharistic fellowship once an appropriate period of penitence was deemed to have been completed. From the early Middle Ages, however, the practice of private and confidential confession to one other person began to spread. By the end of the first millennium, a decisive shift occurred, towards confession of grave sin in confidence to a priest, followed by absolution and suitable acts of penance or 'satisfaction'. From the twelfth century onwards, medieval theology identified such confession as one of the seven sacraments and necessary for salvation in the case of those who had committed mortal (as opposed to venial) sins. That position was confirmed as the teaching of the Roman Catholic Church by the Council of Trent.

Churches of the Protestant Reformation resisted the distinction between mortal and venial sins and the necessity of absolution from a priest, or any human intermediary. Nonetheless, corporate confession of sin became a part of public worship in many cases, and some retained a place for the confession of sins to a minister as an accepted part of pastoral care, including the Church of England. The first Exhortation at Holy Communion contains the words, closely followed in Canon B 29: 'if there be any of you, who by these means cannot quiet his own conscience herein, but requireth further comfort or counsel, let him come to me, or to some discreet and learned minister of God's Word, and open his grief; that by the ministry of God's holy Word he may receive the benefit of absolution, together with ghostly counsel and advice, to the quieting of his conscience and avoiding of all scruple and doubtfulness.' Thus the Protestant Reformation did not challenge and in some respects intensified the medieval Catholic focus on the individual sinner and God, with the relationships between the sinner and the church, and between the sinner and the person sinned against, in danger of fading into the background of the doctrine and the pastoral practice of forgiveness, with regard to the ministry of absolution and much more widely.[55]

The practical implications of this 'hollowing out' of the theology of receiving God's forgiveness have become apparent in the use of the ministry of absolution in the aftermath of abuse.[56] In one of the few in-depth studies carried out of clerical abusers, in this case nine Roman Catholic priests from Ireland, it plays a disturbing role.[57] A significant proportion of the priests experienced, sooner or later, a troubling of their conscience by the abuse they were committing and therefore confessed it in the context of the ministry of absolution. One might expect this to have been a significant moment in their narratives. Yet with one exception, it was not. Confessors did not pass on the knowledge they were holding, even indirectly, to anyone else. Penitents made more or less sincere resolutions to change their behaviour, which did not last. In effect, the ministry of absolution became a kind of pressure release valve for the priests and for the church community that facilitated the perpetuation of child sexual abuse. Cases such as this led to calls for churches that maintain an absolute requirement for priests never to divulge what they are told in this ministry to suspend that requirement in situations pertaining to abuse. A Working Party has been set up to consider whether the Church of England should change its current position on this issue.

The exception to the general picture described in the previous paragraph is, however, worth dwelling on. One of the priests recalls how, after a number of visits to the confessional where he had mentioned acts of abuse, he confessed to a priest who immediately told him with great vehemence that what he had done, as well as being a sin, was a serious crime in the eyes of the law that should be confessed to the police. While the abuser did not in fact do that, the shock of the experience helped to engender a genuine and lasting resolution not to abuse again.

The last confessor the priest faced responded very differently from those he had previously experienced. In part, this was because of the depth of sheer anger and outrage that he evidently communicated. Yet it was also because he did not treat the abuse primarily as a matter of failure to live up to priestly vows of celibacy. Instead, he made it clear that it was a sin not only against God, but also against another human being. There is a fundamental theological truth here: any acknowledgement of a sin against God cannot be given its true sense and weight unless we feel the extent of the damage we have done to others. Only through the injured neighbour can we begin to understand the injury of God.

The corollary, as this incident also implies, is that repentance involves action in the public sphere, not merely an internal resolution against future repetition. Such action needs to include a firm commitment to accept and submit to the exercise of temporal justice by telling the responsible authorities what has happened and accepting the sanctions that may follow, including the imposition of restrictions that restrict the perpetrator's ability to do similar damage in the future. The journey of repentance – which may be lengthy – involves being ready to address the damage done to the abused person and to the wider web of relationships in the church and the community – the 'restorative action' noted above (page 75).

The first point to be made in response to the question for this section is, therefore, that in speaking about God's forgiveness to those who have committed acts of abuse the church needs to draw on the fullness of Christian teaching. Christians have confidence in the power of the proclamation of forgiveness in Christ to change lives. But responding to the good news of forgiveness is properly followed by a readiness to face the consequences of past sin and attend to the restoration of human relationships, while recognizing that those consequences for the sinner may also include weakness of will and deep-seated habits of self-deceit.

The second thing to be said is that the way that the church talks about forgiveness here should also attend to the particular character of the sin. As set out in the first two sections of this document, abuse draws the abuser into a habit of deception that includes self-deception, and a cultivated ability to conceal uncomfortable truths in outward behaviour and obscure them from the abuser's own conscious thinking (pages 35 and 46). In this context it is difficult for repentance to take root in

the whole person. Moreover, repentance that leads the sinner to
seek restoration will necessarily involve public admission of guilt,
barring the one seeking forgiveness from holding the kind of authority
and trust that make abuse possible. Refusal to make such public
admission as a first step in seeking restoration indicates that repentance
has indeed not even begun to take root and therefore that forgiveness
cannot be received – not because God does not offer it, but because
the person involved does not have a heart prepared to accept it.

The discussion of relevant issues in this section would therefore seem
to support the course of action set out in the latest version of the
Guidelines for the Professional Conduct of the Clergy for priests offering
the ministry of absolution. The *Guidelines* state that 'If, in the context of
such a confession, the penitent discloses that he or she has committed
a serious crime, such as the abuse of children or vulnerable adults, the
priest must require the penitent to report his or her conduct to the police
or other statutory authority. If the penitent refuses to do so the priest
should withhold absolution' (paragraph 3.6). The reasoning here would
be that absolute refusal on the part of the penitent to face justice
indicates a failure to recognize the gravity of the sin, and therefore
the absence of penitence, which depends on such recognition.

Although this section has dealt at some length with the ministry
of absolution, it should be understood that the theological parameters
set out here apply in any situation where the church is seeking to speak
of God's forgiveness to those who have committed acts of abuse, either
in the context of such acts being acknowledged by a specific individual,
or simply when a minister is preaching about receiving God's forgiveness.

As has already been noted (page 71), a significant proportion of abusers attend church regularly, and anyone speaking about forgiveness to a church congregation should be aware that there is a possibility that among the hearers is someone conscious of having abused another human being. The idea that their conscience can be relieved without any consequences for their position, status and freedom of action will quite possibly be very welcome news to them, but it is certainly not the good news of God's life-giving forgiveness in Jesus Christ.

In sin, repentance and forgiveness, the relation between the sinner and God is inseparable from the relation between the sinner and other human beings, beginning with the person sinned against and extending (crucially) to the church community of which they are a part. In the case of abuse, the promise of restoration that comes with forgiveness should take some concrete expression in the corporate life of the church, as well as having implications for public acknowledgement and legal process. Very serious issues, however, arise as to what that might mean in practice. As has already been indicated at various points, the promise of God's forgiveness does not carry with it a pledge that so long as there is some evidence of responding to it, the church will simply behave as if nothing happened and take no action with regard to the person who committed the sin. The churches have worked out careful policy guidelines for how those who have committed abuse may participate in congregational life and the restrictions needed here. Some reflection on the theological dimension of this is offered in section 3 of the companion text to this one from the Faith and Order Commission, *The Gospel, Sexual Abuse and the Church: A Theological Resource for the Local Church*, which also contains references to relevant documents.

Fictional Case Study: David

David is a convicted sex offender serving a prison sentence. He has responded well to the opportunities to work through his issues and now realizes how inappropriate his relationship with his teenage daughter's 15-year-old best friend had been. He has also admitted to a history of relationships with underage girls dating back to his early twenties. David has accepted that he cannot return to his wife and family and doesn't want to make life any more difficult for them. On release from prison he will move back to the part of the world where he grew up.

In prison David has participated in a Sex Offender Treatment Programme, which has given him an understanding of how and why he has committed sexual offences, and helped him to develop strategies for coping in situations where he knows he is at risk of re-offending.

David knows that many people cannot forgive him for what he has done – his own family members, the girls he abused and, in the cases where this is known, members of their families. He has enjoyed chapel in prison, where he participated in leading the worship, but doesn't anticipate joining a local church when he leaves. What he wants to know is how he stands with God. Does God forgive, even when all these people remain hurt and angry, and when he feels he can't forgive himself?

General considerations in responding

David needs to be assured that he has come to a good understanding of the situation. His participation in therapeutic programmes is evidence of his good intentions, and what he has learnt, and what he has resolved and decided, is all evidence of sincere and deep repentance.

On release, he could meet with the Diocesan Safeguarding Adviser to discuss whether there is a priest or spiritual director who might continue to give him spiritual support in his journey of faith. He can also be informed of what steps and safeguards would need to be put in place should he wish to attend church in the future. Details of these can be found in the Church of England's national policy document, *Practice Guidance: Risk Assessment.*

Questions about forgiveness and reconciliation

David is clearly very concerned about forgiveness. How much thought has he given to the relationship between repentance and forgiveness? It is clear that he wishes to stop offending, but to what extent is this because he grasps the harm that he has done to others through acts of abuse? What does sincere repentance look like here, when someone has suffered very serious consequences for their actions, consequences they may well sincerely wish to avoid experiencing again? Is it possible that David has been through periods of contrition previously that have proved transient? Does he accept that, even with sincere repentance and assurance of God's grace, he still needs to accept a discipline (e.g. of restricted access to young people) which will help him control his behaviour? Does he recognize that the consequences of his sin may continue to affect all involved, however sincere and deep his repentance?

Why is David concerned with God's forgiveness in particular? Divine forgiveness in the Bible concerns restoration to right relationship with those affected by our sins, both more and less directly, yet it is not clear how strongly this figures on his horizon. It is at the same time about the restoration of communion with God – does David believe that this remains broken in his case? Ultimately, the approach set out in this document would want to say that God's offer of transforming forgiveness indeed stands open, for David as for every human person, but receiving the gift will, by God's grace, draw us onto the road of repentance.

Repentance and forgiveness are inseparable from one another and sometimes demand that the penitent seek justice and undertake restorative action. David has suffered the punishment of the law for what he has done wrong, and appears to be determined not to compound the harm he has done for others once he comes out of prison. He may still, however, want to think about whether there is anything further he could and should do to affirm his welcome of God's forgiveness and his determination to seek first God's kingdom and God's justice.

5. How should the church speak of forgiving to those who have experienced abuse?

The church's primary pastoral task is to listen with care and sensitivity to those who have been abused, supporting them on the road towards healing and in taking steps towards the achievement of temporal justice. Christian ministers should avoid the use of trivializing language about forgiveness which suggests that it is easy, instant or a condition of God's continued love. The words on forgiveness in the Lord's Prayer need to be read as the prayer of the whole church, seeking to be like the Father through the Son in the power of the Spirit, not asserting a claim on God's forgiveness based on our individual performance of it. In real life, forgiveness is rarely a straightforward exchange between victim and perpetrator in which complete repentance is met by complete forgiveness. Rather than being an episode or an event, forgiving is better understood as a long journey or struggle with the claims of justice and mercy, during the course of which forgiveness emerges.

This document seeks to respond to the tension between superficial church teaching on forgiveness and what emerges from listening to survivors. Ordinary preaching and teaching can present forgiveness of others as a prerequisite for receiving God's forgiveness and being able to live by faith in the family of the church. Those who are aware of their own inner resistance to forgiving those who have wronged them are thereby given the message, at least implicitly, that they are not welcome in church, or may even be in danger of losing their salvation. If they admit to such resistance, support may be offered through prayer and pastoral counsel, but if they appear incapable of being able to benefit from it, then the perception may be communicated that they are being disobedient to the will of God and therefore have no secure place in the church.

Survivors of abuse report that this kind of teaching has been deeply destructive for them and may indeed have played a key role in leading them away from the church, if not from Christian faith altogether. They may have no desire to turn towards the person who abused them with the offer of forgiveness, and the instincts against it run very deep; for example, a survivor may not feel safe enough to consider any kind of contact. Moreover, there is anger and perplexity that the church can seem to focus on the responsibility of the victim towards the perpetrator, and their consequent guilt for not acting 'properly' towards him or her by offering instant forgiveness, when in fact the real guilt lies with the perpetrator together with those in responsibility who failed to take action to prevent the abuse, and indeed whose failures may be ongoing. Some would even speak of those who have been abused being re-abused through subjection to such harmful teaching, not least because it may invoke destructive feelings of guilt associated with the original abuse itself (page 45).

The harm may be particularly evident in the context of domestic violence, when forgiving the perpetrator is taken to mean being willing to put oneself back in harm's way.[58] Those who preach and teach need to ask not only whether they would say as much to a victim of domestic violence in pastoral ministry, but also whether a current victim of domestic violence might reasonably reach such a conclusion from hearing them speaking to the congregation about the duty to forgive in general.

Some of the survivors spoken to by the group who drafted this report had a very simple answer to the question for this section: in their view, the church should not speak to those who have been victims of abuse about forgiving abusers at all. For some, this is because it is not relevant; for others, because it cannot be heard when presented as a demand. Some would say that they recognize the 'struggle to forgive': that forgiving is good, important and ultimately even necessary, but in the case of abuse characterized by the four dimensions set out in section 1, forgiveness is hugely challenging, and will always be a struggle, never a simple achievement.[59]

The tension felt by survivors who identify as Christians may crystallize around the Lord's Prayer (Matthew 6.9–15; cf. Luke 11.2–4). A survivor who is a licensed minister in the Church of England said that every time she leads the congregation in saying it, 'I know I am telling a lie,' presumably because she understands the Scripture here to mean that God cannot forgive an individual who has not fully forgiven another individual. Yet this interpretation is deeply questionable.

In Matthew's version, both the portion of the prayer in 6.12 ('And forgive us our debts, as we also have forgiven our debtors'), and Jesus' comments immediately following the prayer in verses 14–15 ('For if you forgive others their trespasses, your heavenly Father will also forgive you; but if you do not forgive others, neither will your Father forgive your trespasses'), focus on the relationship between divine and human forgiveness. It has been suggested that the story of the unforgiving servant (Matthew 18.23–35) is the 'parabolic equivalent' of chapter 6 verses 12, 14 and 15.[60] In this parable, a servant who is forgiven a large debt by his master then refuses to forgive a small debt owed him by a fellow servant. When the master learns of this, he punishes him, revoking forgiveness and demanding full payment. Jesus closes the story by saying, 'So my heavenly Father will also do to every one of you, if you do not forgive your brother or sister from your heart' (18.35). The version of that text in The Message, however, brings out the primary focus of the parable, namely God's abundant mercy: 'That's exactly what my Father in heaven is going to do to each one of you who doesn't forgive unconditionally anyone who asks for mercy.' The lesson for the disciples is not that 'unless you forgive, God cannot forgive you', which would make God's mercy conditional on our actions; rather that in response to God's abundant mercy we should be forgiving to those who ask us for mercy. It is worth noting that the parable concerns how we respond to a person who seeks mercy from us, not how we should relate to someone who does not acknowledge their need for it.

Why should willingness to forgive others matter so much? The gift of divine forgiveness is not for me as an individual in isolation but for every human person, for all humanity, and if I receive the gift I accept with it the possibility that each human person may receive it, including those whose sins against God are bound up with sins against me. The weight of this clause in the Lord's Prayer is on the first part: 'Forgive *us* our sins': not me alone, but all who call God their Father and all whom God wills to do this. If I am prepared to say those words, I cannot remain forever fixed in an attitude of retribution, recrimination or revenge – which is certainly not to say I cannot pray the words while I have some feelings of retribution, recrimination or revenge. I must be open at some level to the gracious gift of God being extended towards those who sin against me, and to its transforming power for them, as also for me in my relation towards them. Being open to this possibility is part of what it means for us to come to accept unconditional love and forgiveness from God, the maker of heaven and earth and the one in whose image every human being is created. It is important to say, of course, that abused people are by no means necessarily fixed in an attitude of retribution, recrimination and revenge. They may wish to be forgiving, but for numerous reasons find it hard, even impossible, at least for the present.

Being open to the possibilities of forgiveness should not be taken to mean that unless Christians can forgive, here and now, all who have sinned against them, God cannot forgive them. To teach this is wrong.

God's love is unconditional and the gift of divine forgiveness is for everyone. Part of the issue here is the highly misleading idea that human forgiveness, above all in the face of sin that inflicts deep trauma, is something that can simply be *done* once and for all, a point that is developed in more detail later in this section. What is asked of those who would pray the Lord's Prayer is that they entrust themselves to the grace of God and acknowledge that this grace has power to enable the hallowing of God's name and the coming of God's reign in every part of their life as earthly creatures, including every relationship woven into it. The text is, after all, a prayer; it is not a statement of fact, but words for what those praying want to be the case. To pray it is not to declare: 'I have forgiven, as God forgives', which would be the most absurd and arrogant presumption; but rather, 'may I become forgiving, may I share in a creaturely way in the divine glory of forgiving, may the grace of God touch me and transform me to be a forgiving person'.

Moreover, it is essential to keep remembering that this is a communal, collective supplication: 'forgive *us our* sins as *we* forgive'. It is a prayer the disciples of Jesus are meant to pray together. When we feel unable to forgive, we can still pray the Lord's Prayer, because it is not an individual prayer, but the prayer of all God's people.[61] Believers are held within the prayer of the whole church, which is encompassed in the whole Christ, Christ in head and members, to use Augustine's terminology. Christ prays for his members what they cannot pray for themselves, so the first and last question for believers is whether they will let themselves be drawn into his intercession for the whole church and the whole world; for the prayer of the Christian is always participation in the prayer of the whole church in Christ and not an autonomous, individual act. The point is not that each individual must be completely and perfectly forgiving, but that the church must be a community committed to forgiveness and reconciliation as inherent aspects of the way of discipleship. To be a Christian, therefore, involves belonging to a body that prays for the coming of the reign of God, knowing that this will include the acceptance of the divine gift of forgiveness beyond sin and therefore life beyond death.

The New Testament does not single out willingness to forgive others as the single, decisive sign of embracing God's forgiveness. The story at Luke 7.41–50, of the anonymous woman who anoints Jesus' feet, also deals with the consequences of forgiveness. The situation of the woman who has been forgiven much is presented in similar terms to the unmerciful servant: a debtor who cannot pay. Having been forgiven the debt, however, her transformation is not seen primarily in forgiving others (for example, those who look down on her at the dinner party), but in the extravagance of her loving response to Jesus, with its shocking lack of concern for social proprieties. Indeed, there is surely a note of warning here for preachers and teachers who present a picture of forgiveness in which they find it easy (too easy?) to locate themselves, and by which they may then pronounce judgement on those whose response to the abundance of God's grace takes a different path.

Two Christians who have walked the hard path of forgiveness and written and spoken publicly about their journey along it are the Revd Lesley Bilinda, whose Rwandan husband was killed in the genocide in Rwanda in 1994, and Fr Michael Lapsley, who lost both his hands and the sight of one eye as the result of a parcel bomb sent to him during the apartheid years in South Africa. While neither suffered abuse directly as it has been characterized here, their experiences graphically illustrate the utter inadequacy of versions of Christian teaching that expect all victims of human sin to be able to offer complete forgiveness to those who have sinned against them following a brief pause for reflection.

To begin with, both Bilinda and Lapsley focus on how the survivor can set out on a journey towards forgiveness, rather than assuming that there is some simple route to the destination where it can be declared and shared with the perpetrator. Bilinda describes four choices that helped her to begin. The first was to acknowledge the reality and horror of what had happened and to accept and take ownership of the strong feelings involved. The second was to choose not to seek revenge or retaliation for what had been done, and the third was to make 'a recognition of the common humanity that I share with the one who has wronged me'.[62] The fourth and final choice was to believe that, with God's help, the perpetrator could turn their life around and live for peace.

For some survivors of abuse, just making the first choice Bilinda mentions may be a significant challenge that takes many years. Lapsley speaks of the work of healing that is often a vital first stage: 'In many cases the messed-upness that we carry has to be addressed before forgiveness and reconciliation can be on the table,' he observes. 'Especially for those who have been deeply traumatized and are fearful, having a secure space that will not be violated is very important. So this, then, begins the process of healing, which for most people is the starting point of a journey that may or may not end in forgiveness.'[63] The need for a secure space is worth underlining. Because of the imbalance of power involved in abuse, as long as that power remains real in the world of interpersonal relations, whether because of the abuser's actual position or because of the emotional scars or indeed both, there is real danger in asking the survivor to forgive their abuser.

The journey of forgiveness needs to begin from a place of safety, physically and psychologically. As it unfolds, it requires the fuller remembrance of the sin that was suffered, the wrong that was done – Bilinda's first choice. Wherever there has been shattering harm, this too is a difficult and potentially dangerous step, and the self has its times and seasons that should be respected. The significant and developing literature on the dynamics of trauma and recovery from it is relevant here (see section 2, page 46 above). Recovery of memory may be blocked in part or whole by a mechanism of self-protection, the self shielding itself from overwhelming feelings associated with the memory. As Lapsley says of people who come to the institute he set up, 'When we tell them they must forgive while they are still in the midst of great pain, we add to their burden.'[64]

The fact that survivors of abuse may experience strong feelings of guilt as these memories return means that before the question of forgiving those who have sinned against them can even be framed, full and truthful remembrance has to establish that they *have* been sinned against, are not 'the bad ones' and do not somehow deserve such suffering (see page 45 in section 2 above). Feelings of guilt may be bound up with feelings of self-contempt, or shame. Writing in the different psychological register of the ancient world, Augustine of Hippo acknowledged that victims of rape often felt a pervasive sense of moral impurity as a result of what had happened to them, arguing forcefully that people need to know this is not true and be released from the burdens it places on them.[65] In such circumstances, the work of truthful remembrance is a prerequisite to the recovery of a proper sense of self, as the gift of the faithful creator.

A place of safety and recovery of memory are essential to the psychological act of 'letting go' of the wrong that has been suffered. It is a demanding step further from this to what might be called interpersonal forgiveness – offering forgiveness to the person who wronged you. For Lapsley, such forgiveness is not even a possibility, for he does not know who sent the bomb. He imagines a scenario, however, in which he meets the person who sent him the bomb that maimed him:

> If one day someone rings my bell and when I open the door says, 'I'm the person who sent you the letter bomb. Will you forgive me?' Now for the first time, forgiveness is on the table. What do I say, yes, no, not yet? What I might say is, 'Excuse me, sir, do you still make letter bombs?' If the person were to say, 'Oh no, actually I work at the local children's hospital,' then I might say, 'Yes, of course I forgive you.' However, what follows in my imaginary scenario is important. As we sit and drink tea

together, I would say, 'Though I have forgiven you, I still
have no hands. I still have only one eye and my eardrums are
damaged. I will live forever with the consequences of what
you did, which means that I will need assistance for the rest
of my life. Of course you will help pay for that, not as a condition
of forgiveness, but as a part of reparation and restitution in
a way that is possible.'[66]

As with God's forgiveness for humanity, so with forgiveness between
human persons: it is offered in the hope that it will meet with
repentance – either repentance that has already been expressed,
or repentance that will follow from the offer of forgiveness itself.
Without repentance, the offer of forgiveness cannot be accepted;
the gift remains waiting to be received. Moreover, repentance includes
willingness to address the present consequences of the penitent's
past action; repentance demands that we attend to the claims of
justice. The dimensions of betrayed trust and of pervasive deceit
in abuse make such a meeting of gift and acceptance particularly
challenging, and often extremely unlikely.

In light of this brief survey it is not surprising that Cherry suggests
that the only true forgiveness is forgiveness that emerges when it has
seemed to be impossible.[67] Above all, the pastoral priority must be to
understand, empathize and share in the grief and anger of individuals,
with an appreciation that every story is different. As Aquinas suggests in
his comments on the Lord's Prayer, forgiveness is the church's corporate
narrative, the word that ultimately describes the unfolding divine plot in

which we find ourselves together, but it is made up of many narratives and they proceed in different ways, each with its share of impasse and grief, and each with its own miracles and surprises. Lapsley's practice of giving opportunities for survivors of abuse to work together through what they make of forgiveness in their own situation provides a practical example of how the church can nurture forgiveness in the aftermath of abuse, in a way that is empowering and that resists the individualization of forgiveness. While there are serious theoretical and theological questions to be addressed, actual forgiveness between real people needs to be worked out afresh on each occasion and cannot be controlled or predicted from outside.

To forgive another person involves a particular kind of empathy: to know them in their sin and even have some sense of their perspective on that sin, while also grasping the hope of life that is not determined by that sin, for both perpetrator and victim. This corresponds with the way of divine forgiveness, shown to us in the incarnation and death on the cross of the Son of God, tempted in every way as we are and made sin for our sake (2 Corinthians 5.21). While forgiveness between people is not simply homologous with God's forgiveness of us, it nevertheless participates in the same theological dynamic, including this difficult journey of empathy.[68] There are parallels here with Bilinda's four stages, in particular the third, recognition of common humanity, and the fourth, belief that it is possible for the perpetrator to receive grace and newness of life: both require some kind of empathy if they are not to be merely abstract, theoretical beliefs. This is part of the cost of forgiving, which is related to the costliness of repentance, as responses to the heavy price of sin.

Applying these insights in the context of abuse as defined here brings real problems. One thing we know about those who have abused others is that they have exploited their interpersonal or positional power, and in many if not all cases, this has involved manipulating the feelings of the abused. That this habit or pattern may continue is a significant possibility. Unless it is based on mature theology, preaching, teaching and pastoral counselling on forgiveness and reconciliation may actually encourage the perpetuation of abuse. This is especially so when it comes to the matter of empathy. Encouraging the abused to establish empathy should not be considered until the steps of finding a place of safety and recovering truthful remembrance that breaks the hold of guilt and shame have been taken. Some of those responsible for abuse may not even be known to the survivor, for instance in the case of pornography involving children or the coercion of vulnerable adults. They may be dead by the time the survivor is ready to consider these matters. Yet ultimately it is hard to see how forgiveness in the interpersonal sense that is the focus here can be completed unless the abused person somehow comes to the point where they are able to face the perpetrator, without either minimizing the wrong done or demonizing the one who did it. The aim is to recognize a human being who is made in the image of God, and whose humanity is bound up with my own, in the sinful, disfigured face of the abuser. Forgiveness, however, does not need to be complete to be real.

Fictional Case Study: Darren

Darren suffered sexual abuse between the ages of 10 and 12 from a member of the clergy who has recently been convicted for these and other offences. Darren is now 25 and showing classic symptoms of PTSD. He feels terribly guilty about the abuse, and is now feeling suicidal because of a sense of shame that won't go away. He wants to be able to forgive himself but can't.

General considerations in responding

Darren needs to be assured that his feelings are to be expected for someone who has been abused, but that he is not to blame for the abuse, and was not responsible for it. He needs therapeutic clinical support in order to work through his feelings before he considers forgiveness, either of himself or of his abuser, alongside reassurance that there are people in the church who can be trusted to listen to him and walk alongside him.

Questions to ask Darren:
- Does Darren feel safe enough talking to me?
- What support has he received, and what is he currently receiving?
- Who is funding this – and is there a clear offer for the church to pay for what he needs, as his abuse was by a priest?

- To what extent does he recognize himself as a victim, who is not to blame, and how can the church help him to recognize its own responsibility for the abuse?
- How has the abuse affected his relationship with God (i.e. spiritual abuse)?
- How does he now feel about the church? Does he attend church? What does he want, and who might help him, on his own faith journey?

Questions about forgiveness and reconciliation

There is no notion of 'forgiving oneself' in Christian theological tradition, but that is the place where Darren finds himself struggling. Moreover, it seems obvious that Darren has no need to be forgiven by himself, or anyone else, for his abuse: he was the person abused, so the only forgiving he might do is of the perpetrator. It could seem that the only way therefore to draw on theology in communicating with Darren is to dismiss his perspective, which would clearly be unhelpful. Are there ways in which the church can address the harrowing feelings of shame and pollution he may be experiencing, while nonetheless affirming that he does not carry guilt before God for what was done to him? Is it not rather Darren's sense of distance from God that is calling for assurance and deep acceptance?

Darren's situation is a reminder that the question of forgiveness is generally the wrong place to start with survivors of abuse in a church context. Not because it does not matter, but because it can only begin to come into focus at all when other aspects of the situation have been addressed. In particular, the person who has been abused needs to feel secure from the risk of further abuse, and the perpetrator needs to be brought to justice. In traumatic cases like Darren's, there must be opportunity for what Lapsley calls 'the healing of memories' to take place – a process that may take many years. Without such healing, there can be no true perception of what has happened, and therefore no fruitful response to it.

Fifteen centuries ago, Augustine of Hippo recognized the way that sexual violation could create an almost unbearable sense of shame, leading victims to harbour deep feelings of guilt and self-loathing. More recent psychology might add to this the understanding that holding oneself responsible can be a way of shielding the self from the still more painful reality of utter helplessness and vulnerability. All of this underlines the need for pastors not to get in the way of the professional, therapeutic support that Darren may need with unhelpful simplifications of biblical teaching.

What might the positive role of the church and its ministry be in this context? Would a formal, face-to-face apology for the abuse, from the diocesan bishop, help him to move forward on his journey? If Darren remains part of, or in contact with, the parish where he was abused, what might he need to hear from them – and what might they benefit by hearing from him?

6. Does the church have a ministry of reconciliation in the aftermath of abuse?

Reconciliation has many dimensions. One expression of reconciliation is the face-to-face meeting of the people involved. The hope of ultimate reconciliation in Christ is a distinctive hope of the church, but the implied resumption of relationship with the abuser can be disturbing for those who have suffered traumatic and shattering consequences of abuse and is certainly not something that should be forced on a survivor of abuse. Any intentional steps towards some kind of formal reconciliation, including (in this context) various forms of restorative practice, must be fully respectful of the survivor of abuse and their wishes. For all the challenges here, there will be cases where movement towards reconciliation may be possible. They are most likely to be situations where temporal justice has been exercised, healing is a reality for the abused, and the abuser's repentance leads to reform. The church's ministry of reconciliation in the aftermath of abuse is primarily demonstrated in seeking for these things, rather than in facilitating the reconciliation process as such, especially when the church has been involved in the abuse in some way.

For Paul, 'reconciliation' provides a lens through which God's relationship with the world can be viewed and interpreted (2 Corinthians 5.18–21).[69] Indeed, it has recently been argued that reconciliation is central for the theology of Paul if not the New Testament as a whole.[70] Following his teaching, reconciliation at its heart is God reaching out in the person of Jesus Christ in order to restore and renew the fractured relationship between God and humanity. This work of reconciliation finds its centre at the cross, where the one who knew no sin is made sin for our sake (2 Corinthians 5.21). God's reconciliation with humanity through the cross may then be understood to feed all other acts of reconciliation.

Many would want to stress the connection between God's presence in Christ reconciling the world to himself, and the church's ministry of reconciliation as a calling for all Christians to be peacemakers and to be involved in bringing together those who have been divided from one another by fear, mistrust and violence. Christians have been in the forefront of those leading and shaping intentional processes of reconciliation in South Africa and Northern Ireland (though it also has to be acknowledged that Christians have their share of responsibility for the divisions in those places). Within the Church of England, Coventry Cathedral has developed a distinctive international ministry of reconciliation with origins in the response to the Second World War. Archbishop Justin Welby, who once served as a Canon there, has made reconciliation one of the three priorities for his ministry as Archbishop. On the face of things, therefore, Christians should be committed to seeking reconciliation in the aftermath of abuse. Abuse, as characterized by the four parameters set out in the first section, destroys relationships of trust at a fundamental level. Many victims will respond to the shattering harm it causes by putting as much distance as possible between themselves and those who abused them. The move from understanding themselves as a 'victim' to a 'survivor' may well involve being able to articulate profound anger towards the abuser, as well as towards those who held responsibility for preventing the abuse and for dealing with the abuser but failed in that responsibility. Moreover, as noted in section 2, bystanders who recognize abuse for what it is may also be enraged. Such rage can become destructive. The fear and loathing it generates may leave people unable to acknowledge the continuing humanity of the perpetrator, or endure their presence in the community.

One might therefore presume that the church's ministry of reconciliation is precisely what is needed in response to the poisoning of so many relationships through the sin of abuse. Only reconciliation, it might seem, can bring peace for and between victim, perpetrator, those with responsibility and those who found themselves as bystanders. Yet in the light of what has been said in the text so far, real questions have to be asked about this.

To begin with, as noted in section 3, the church as institution has in some cases been involved in the abuse as a body holding responsibilities for prevention and proper response. In such circumstances, people identified with it cannot easily be agents of reconciliation. In many more cases, the church community will include a number who are bystanders in one way or another, some disbelieving that a person convicted of abuse could ever have acted in such a way, some demanding that they be punished and some trying to avoid the situation (and the conflict it generates) completely. Even where the original abuse was not linked to a church context, survivors may be mistrustful of the church, both because of their own experiences of inadequate pastoral ministry and teaching in similar situations and because of the wider public record of the churches in failing to deal properly with abuse. They may have left the church, with no wish to re-engage.

Moreover, reconciliation, both with their abuser and with those who have been in some way complicit in enabling the abuse to happen, or subsequently protecting the abuser, is simply not on the horizon for many survivors. There are many reasons for this, but we must reckon with the depth of the damage done through abuse. It takes time (measured in decades) for some survivors to come to the point where they can even make the initial step, identified (in varying terms) by Bilinda and Lapsley in the previous section, of fully acknowledging to themselves and others what took place and the effect it has had on them (pages 91–3 above). By this point, the abuser may be dead or on the other side of the world. Indeed, it may be news of their death that finally leaves the survivor feeling safe enough to face what was done to them. On the other hand, it may open up new feelings of ambiguity and distress.

Reconciliation takes various forms and can be understood in different ways, but the approach being taken here is one of restoration of relationship that has both a divine–human dimension and a human–human dimension. In the aftermath of grave sin, such restoration cannot ultimately bypass questions of interpersonal forgiveness. Reconciliation, on this model, depends on the willingness of the person who has been wronged to enter a process in which forgiveness may, at some point, be offered and perhaps received. As was made clear in the previous section, to expect survivors of abuse to offer such forgiveness, with the implication of some kind of weakness or failure if they are unable to, is wrong. By trying to initiate reconciliation in the aftermath of abuse, the church may be doing immense damage to those for whom it should be seeking to care. Any moves towards a process of reconciliation need to begin with the free choice and settled decision of the abused person.[71]

Repentance may in some circumstances follow from, rather than precede, the astonishing gift of forgiveness, for instance in the case of Saul/Paul in Acts 9.1–19 and 22.6–21; the stories in the Gospels of Zacchaeus (Luke 19.1–10) and the woman caught in adultery might also be noted here (John 8.1–11). Repentance cannot, however, be kept out of the picture, as was emphasized in section 4. Being forgiven, like forgiving, implies a full remembrance and recognition of the wrong that was done. Yet the practices of deceit implicit in abuse erode the capacity to speak and act truthfully. What kind of repentance, then, can be expected? What kind of repentance could be hoped for?

At the very least, repentance in this context must involve a visible surrender of the power and authority that were used to perpetrate the abuse, as a direct consequence of acknowledging the seriousness of the moral wrong. Reconciliation, in any context, depends on right timing.[72] Reconciliation cannot take place in the midst of a crisis, for instance, but only once it is over, and the demands of temporal justice have been honoured and, as far as possible, met. In the particular situation of the aftermath of abuse, reconciliation cannot begin to be considered until the person who has been abused is given the safety they need and has recovered significantly from the harm inflicted. This is likely to be particularly challenging in a situation of domestic violence where the couple remain together and living under the same roof, perhaps as members of the same church congregation.

There is, therefore, a need for very great care in speaking of the church's ministry of reconciliation. Yet there are remarkable stories that can give hope. To take a recent example, in May 2015 Eva Kor was called to give evidence against 94-year-old former SS officer Oskar Groening, on trial for accessory to the murder of 300,000 prisoners at Auschwitz. A survivor of Auschwitz, Kor and her twin sister Miriam had been objects of Mengele's horrendous medical experiments. Kor told Groening during the trial that she forgave him any wrongdoing, but added that her forgiveness did not absolve the perpetrator from taking responsibility for his actions. When she had finished giving evidence, she accepted an embrace from him, a physical sign of reconciliation after the physical torture she received from his hands. It was a powerful action but also a disturbing one, when recalled in this context, and it invites further questions.

Was this reconciliation real? Perhaps it was, but to give an affirmative answer it would be necessary to know something about Groening as well as Kor in that moment. Was his move to embrace her an implicit gesture of repentance, recognizing the wrong he had done and acknowledging his need for her forgiveness, or was it really about something else? Reconciliation takes place between the people involved, and therefore cannot lie wholly in the power of any one of them.

The courtroom setting of this encounter may also remind us that reconciliation concerns justice; it cannot undo the past, but it does involve addressing the wrongs that have been done and setting relationships right in the present. As was stressed earlier in this document, the good news of God contains the promise of justice (section 3, pages 63–4 above), which cannot be opposed to the gracious offer of forgiveness. Moreover, reconciliation is not simply about the relationship between victim and perpetrator as two individuals in isolation, but also about those who held various kinds of responsibility within the situation where the abuse occurred, and those who can be described more loosely as bystanders: those who knew what was happening at the time, those who have come to know about it and those affected by it.

Reconciliation, then, cannot be separated from justice, including the proper exercise of 'temporal' justice in enabling the truth to be told and acknowledged, wrongdoing punished and the vulnerable protected. There has been much interest in 'restorative justice' as a model of justice complementary to that of the law, and in particular interest from churches as to how it might relate to theological perspectives on responding to wrongdoing.[73] One version of restorative justice involves bringing someone who has harmed another (through an action which is both criminal and traumatizing) together with the person they have harmed. The hoped-for outcomes include sensitizing the offender to the personal damage done, with a view to helping them prepare for life in normal society. Sometimes there are also hopes of restoring positive relationship between the offender and the victim. It is possible that forgiveness could be a fruit of the process, but it does not start from or depend on it.[74] Only if there is some meeting of the journeys towards justice, repentance (on the part of the perpetrator) and forgiveness (on the part of the survivor) can we begin to see reconciliation of the kind that is being envisaged here taking shape at the level of human relationships.

There are clear dangers in seeking to adopt a restorative justice approach in the case of abuse. The victim may well not feel safe enough; they can be made vulnerable once again, and the perpetrator may be able to exploit the situation for further abuse. Moreover, the nature of abuse is such that the process is likely to need to draw in those who have been involved as people with responsibility, as well as some at least from the broader category of bystanders, if it is to be truly effective. This may quickly become a complex and even controversial undertaking.

Nonetheless, a case can be made for churches being open to the possibility of some form of restorative practice, while always remaining alert to these very serious challenges.[75] It was said in section 4 that 'receiving God's forgiveness cannot be divorced from repentance that is ready to seek restoration of relationships at the level of human community. This repentance can be demonstrated through 'restorative action' (page 75) with regard both to those who have been wronged (so Zacchaeus) and also to those with whom there is a common life of holiness in Christ, which has been wounded by their actions (so 1 Corinthians 5.1–5).' It therefore belongs to the church's ministry of reconciliation to ask at an appropriate point what such restorative action might mean in the aftermath of abuse and to assist in enabling it, recognizing that this is by no means all that justice requires and certainly cannot be used as a substitute for legal proceedings. Indeed, as was argued in section 4, willingness to face criminal prosecution may be a critical first step to restorative action here.

Moreover, insofar as the church itself recognizes a need to repent, as discussed in section 3, the church also has to ask what kind of restorative action it might be called to undertake in the aftermath of abuse. Without denying the appropriateness of separate responses to that call from various people and institutions involved in a situation of abuse, there may be a case for framing a process of 'restorative practice' that brings them together and helps them to face one another, as well as those who have been harmed by the abuse itself, so long as the vital conditions underlined on pages 104–6 above have been met. Such a process may enable restorative action that carries far more weight than individual initiatives in expressing repentance and in repairing relationships, as part of the road to reconciliation.

The church hopes and prays for reconciliation. Its ministry of reconciliation comes from the gift of God in Christ, who is our peace and who unites those who were estranged from one another in his new humanity (Ephesians 2.14-19). In the immediate aftermath of abuse, however, the focus of Christians should be elsewhere: safety for victims, reducing risks of recurrence and ensuring that anyone against whom there is credible evidence of guilt faces temporal justice. Then attention needs to be given to what healing may mean for survivors – a secure space being the essential context in which feelings of guilt and shame may begin to be addressed, memories begin to be healed and relationships begin to be restored. When these things have happened, there may eventually come a time when reconciliation does not appear impossible, and survivors can decide to face the risks involved in beginning to test that perception against reality.

While great care is undoubtedly needed in this area, the church remains the one body of Christ, to which survivors, perpetrators, those who have failed in their responsibilities and those caught up in the aftermath of abuse may all belong; it is not closed to any of those involved in abuse, in whatever way. The church, therefore, has the potential to shape a space in which reconciliation may, however falteringly, take place. Listening to survivors must be at the heart of this. Only as and when survivors of abuse may choose to initiate them can any practical steps towards reconciliation involving perpetrators be taken (pages 104-5). Many survivors continue to be estranged from, and deeply angry with, the church itself, and a church that is attending to this knows that it has to be a penitent participant in any kind of reconciliation process here, not the primary agent or the facilitator. In parallel with what was said at the end of the last section, caring about reconciliation may best be expressed without focusing directly on reconciliation. The primary imperative for the church in the aftermath of abuse is to strive for justice to be done, healing to become real for the person abused, and repentance to be reforming for the abuser and those who have collaborated or colluded with the abuse in any way. This is the best course by which it can prepare the way for Christ's ministry of reconciliation.

Fictional Case Study: Andrew and Jody

Andrew is separated from his wife, Jody, who had called the police and had him arrested after an incident of domestic abuse. Charges were pressed, and he was found guilty and given a community service order. Andrew is living apart from Jody. The couple have two children aged 6 and 8, both of whom live with Jody. Andrew wants to be reconciled with his wife and with the church of which they are both long-standing members. He has come to the vicarage to discuss this with the vicar, whom he asks to run an informal 'truth and reconciliation' meeting for anyone in the church who wants to come, in which he can explain what he has done, how sorry he is and how he is desperate to be re-integrated into his two homes – his domestic home and his spiritual home. He is currently not attending church.

General considerations in responding

Any consideration of reconciliation with Jody must take heed to assess the risks to her and to their children, and can only be considered if Jody is also willing to consider a conciliation process.

The vicar should not get involved in any conciliation between them as this is specialist work and needs to be undertaken by an independent agency equipped for the purpose. The vicar can signpost Andrew to such agencies.

The vicar needs to be aware of boundaries of confidentiality, and should not be passing information from Andrew to Jody or vice versa. If he or she were to do so not only may they lose the trust of one or the other, but may also be putting Jody at further risk.

The vicar should take care not to prioritize the sanctity of marriage over the safety of vulnerable people.

Questions about forgiveness and reconciliation

Reconciliation in Christian theology is linked to both forgiveness and repentance. What evidence is there of Andrew's repentance, expressed in concrete acts of restoration and commitment to changed behaviour and sustained over a period of time? What insight does he have into the effects of his action?

The fact that the vicar knows both Andrew and Jody has an effect on what he can and cannot do in this situation. There is an obvious danger of him being more or less consciously manipulated by Andrew to support him. If Andrew is serious about showing repentance and receiving God's forgiveness, it would be best if the vicar can identify a priest or pastor not known to them both with whom he can meet regularly. Might there also be a case for Andrew worshipping with a different congregation for a while?

The situation underlines the point that while reconciliation is at the heart of the church's life, this does not mean that its leaders, communities and institutions are always best placed to set up and facilitate a formal process of reconciliation. In this context, the key role of the church may be to pass on the request to an independent agency, which may not have any form of Christian affiliation. If Andrew and Jody do decide to work towards reconciliation, however, and to be part of the church community as they do so, then the church will inevitably be part of the process in one way or another. What might its role be in this situation? How might it witness to the gospel of reconciliation in the context of a 'secular' reconciliation process?

It is clear that there can be no move towards reconciliation unless and until Jody is willing to initiate it. How much is that bound up with her willingness to forgive Andrew? Can there be reconciliation between people without forgiveness? If both reconciliation and forgiveness are processes, does there need to be some kind of synchronization between them?

How does reconciliation between Andrew and Jody relate to their reconciliation with God through Jesus Christ? How does reconciliation with God shape a distinctively Christian approach to reconciliation with other people?

Conclusion

This document has sought to address some of the critical questions that confront Christians seeking to speak and act in the aftermath of abuse in a way that is faithful to the gospel.

The gospel is good news, but for people who have experienced serious, even shattering harm – the first of the dimensions of abuse identified here – failures in preaching, teaching and pastoral guidance may easily obscure that. There is no short-cut to healing, and for the person struggling to recover from such harm, the message that forgiving and being reconciled with their abuser is a condition for receiving the good news can only be expected to be received as bad news, a stone instead of bread (cf. Matthew 7.9). The other dimensions of abuse noted in this document – imbalance of power, betrayal of trust and habits of deceit on the part of the perpetrator, including self-deceit – intensify the difficulties and indeed grave dangers here for attempts towards the restoration of relationships implicit in the Christian tradition and explicit in its understanding of reconciliation. Underestimating the capacity of abusers to manipulate the trust of Christians with claims of repentance has helped to keep doors open to continuing abuse in the church, which is good news to no one.

To acknowledge this is not, however, to conclude that the aftermath of abuse renders the gospel irrelevant, or creates a situation where the call for repentance and forgiveness must be set aside because of more pressing imperatives. Rather, it should make us think more carefully about the meaning both of forgiveness and of reconciliation in the light of God's revelation to us. It is the truth that sets us free (John 8.32): if the gospel of forgiveness is true, then it is liberation for all at all times, not just for some or some of the time.

A certain cheapening of the doctrine of forgiveness lies at the root of a number of the issues analysed in this document, and is not confined to one part of the spectrum of contemporary Christianity. Such a tendency has no patience with the note of struggle that has to be heard in both forgiving and being forgiven after shattering harm, nor with the time that such struggle may take, and the potential need for it to be measured in decades, rather than weeks or months. In such contexts, the idea that the words 'I forgive you' can and should be immediately invoked to effect instantaneous, complete and permanent change is a naive and damaging illusion. There is a corresponding and deeply pernicious illusion in the idea that the words 'I am sorry for what I have done' in the aftermath of abuse may mark a decision so transforming as to allow all concerned to act as if the offence had never occurred. That is not to say that such words may not be spoken with sincerity and truth, but when that first happens they will mark a gracious moment in a long and demanding process, and not the end of the matter so far as the church is concerned.

The church teaches that God's forgiveness and God's reconciliation are both utterly free and infinitely costly: utterly free in that we cannot make any contribution towards it, infinitely costly in the figure of the lamb slain before the foundation of the world (Revelation 13.8). While we cannot offer anything towards it, neither can we receive it without being changed, without being willing to lose our life and die with Christ so that we might live with him.

Forgiving and being forgiven both hinge on recognizing the sin that has been committed and its gravity: not only recalling and acknowledging what has happened, but knowing it as sin, as a radically destructive act against human beings that separates from God and binds to the darkness, yet darkness in which Christ, the light of the world, still shines – a light even the world's deepest darkness cannot overcome (John 1.5). In the aftermath of abuse, being faithful to the gospel of forgiveness means enabling people to come to a place where it becomes possible to see what has happened in that light, including the reality of sin and suffering. For those who have suffered abuse, this must begin (but only begin) with finding a place of safety and with companionship, care and support. For those who have committed abuse, it begins with laying down the power that has been misused to commit the abuse, admitting what they have done to the police and other relevant authorities, facing justice and receiving the punishment and sanctions that then follow. None of this is opposed to forgiveness, but rather shapes the space in which the possibility of that gift may emerge, and the good news be received.

Notes

1. *Working Together to Safeguard Children: A Guide to Inter-agency Working to Safeguard and Promote the Welfare of Children* (HM Government, 2015). The contemporary use of the phrase 'child abuse' apparently dates from 1961, when it was used to refer to what we would call physical abuse. 'Child sexual abuse' then emerges as the preferred way to refer to adult–child sexual contact in the 1970s, according to Marie Keenan, *Child Sexual Abuse and the Catholic Church: Gender, Power, and Organizational Culture* (Oxford: Oxford University Press, 2012), pp. 99–101.
2. Archbishops' Council, *Protecting All God's Children: The Policy for Safeguarding Children in the Church of England*, 4th ed. (London: Church House Publishing, 2010), e.g. 1.11, 1.21 and 3.10ff. Archbishops' Council, *Responding to Domestic Abuse: Policy and Practice Guidance* (2017) cites another government document's definition of domestic abuse, which distinguishes psychological, physical, sexual, financial and emotional abuse (pp. 25–26).
3. *Protecting All God's Children*, 3.34–5; *Responding to Domestic Abuse*, pp. 5 and 26; Archbishops' Council, *Promoting a Safe Church: Policy for Safeguarding Adults in the Church of England* (Church House Publishing 2006), A2.2; Archbishops' Council, *Responding Well to Those Who Have Been Sexually Abused: Policy and Guidance for the Church of England* (London: Church House Publishing, 2011), B.12.
4. *Responding Well*, B.13–14, C.4; *Responding to Domestic Abuse,* p. 26.
5. Maria Mayo, *The Limits of Forgiveness: Case Studies in the Distortion of a Biblical Ideal* (Minneapolis: Fortress Press, 2015).
6. L. Gregory Jones, *Embodying Forgiveness: A Theological Analysis* (Grand Rapids: Eerdmans, 1995); Miroslav Volf, *Exclusion and Embrace: A Theological Exploration of Identity, Otherness, and Reconciliation* (Nashville: Abingdon, 1996).
7. Anthony Bash, *Forgiveness and Christian Ethics* (Cambridge: Cambridge University Press, 2007); Stephen Cherry, *Healing Agony: Re-imagining Forgiveness* (London: Continuum, 2012). Bash has written a number of other books on forgiveness, including *Just Forgiveness: Exploring the Bible, Weighing the Issues* (London: SPCK, 2011), and *Forgiveness: A Theology* (Eugene: Cascade, 2015).
8. Archbishop Desmond Tutu, *No Future Without Forgiveness* (New York: Doubleday, 1999) and, with Rev Mpho Tutu, *The Book of Forgiving: The Fourfold Path for Healing Ourselves and the World* (London: Collins, 2014).
9. Donald W. Shriver, *An Ethic for Enemies: Forgiveness in Politics* (Oxford: Oxford University Press, 1995).
10. Marina Cantacuzino, *The Forgiveness Project: Stories for a Vengeful Age* (London: Jessica Kingsley, 2015); Kate Kellaway, 'Can You Forgive the Unforgivable?', *Observer*, 25 June 2006, available at

http://www.theguardian.com/theobserver/2006/jun/25/features.review17 (accessed 15/07/17).

11. Cantacuzino, *Forgiveness Project*. See also Bash, *Forgiveness: A Theology*, pp. 58–62.

12. Tutu in *No Future Without Forgiveness* argues for forgiveness with or without repentance; cf. Bash in *Forgiveness and Christian Ethics*.

13. See Bash, *Just Forgiveness*.

14. For a detailed discussion of the nature of the work of judgement, see Oliver O'Donovan, *The Ways of Judgement* (Grand Rapids: Eerdmans, 2005), esp. chapter 1.

15. For a discussion of the grounding of justice in human worth, see Nicholas Wolterstorff, *Justice: Rights and Wrongs* (Princeton: Princeton University Press, 2008). For a concise overview, see Joshua Hordern, 'Justice: Rights and Wrongs. An overview', *Studies in Christian Ethics*, 23:2 (2010), pp. 118–29.

16. One might keep in mind another woman in the Scriptures named Tamar when reading this passage, the daughter-in-law of Judah whose story is told in Genesis 38.

17. Gerald West and Phumzile Zondi-Mabizela, 'The Bible Story that Became a Campaign: The Tamar Campaign in South Africa (and beyond),' *Ministerial Formation*, July 2004, http://ujamaa.ukzn.ac.za/Files/the%20bible%20story.pdf (accessed 7/1/2015).

18. The choice of terminology is influenced by Cherry's use of 'shattering hurt' in *Healing Agony*.

19. Keenan, *Child Sexual Abuse*, p. 169.

20. See e.g. the third from last paragraph in the 'Principles' set out in slightly different formats at the start of *Protecting All God's Children* and *Responding Well*; also further comments in *Protecting All God's Children*, 2.17–19 and *Promoting a Safe Church*, p. 38. *Responding to Domestic Abuse* asserts that 'domestic abuse is caused by a misuse of power by one person over another' (p. 31).

21. It is worth noting that an early and influential contribution to theological reflection on safeguarding and sexual abuse placed the abuse of power at the centre of its analysis: James Newton Poling, *The Abuse of Power: A Theological Problem* (Nashville: Abingdon, 1991).

22. On power as an 'essentially contested concept', that always 'arises out of and operates within a particular moral and political perspective', see Steven Lukes, *Power: A Radical View*, 2nd ed. (Basingstoke: Palgrave Macmillan, 2005), pp. 29–30.

23. E.g. Stephen Sykes, *Power and Christian Theology* (London: Continuum, 2006); Kathy Ehrensperger, *Paul and the Dynamics of Power: Communication and Interaction in the Early Christ-Movement* (London: T & T Clark, 2007).

24. Phyllis Trible, *Texts of Terror: Literary-Feminist Readings of Biblical Narratives* (Philadelphia: Fortress Press, 1984), p. 50.
25. John W. Martens, '"Do Not Sexually Abuse Children": The Language of Early Christian Sexual Ethics', in Cornelia B. Horn and Robert R. Phoenix (eds.), *Children in Late Ancient Christianity* (Tübingen: Mohr Siebeck, 2009), pp. 227–54.
26. Keenan, *Child Sexual Abuse*.
27. Alistair McFadyen, *Bound to Sin* (Cambridge: Cambridge University Press, 2000), pp. 57–8.
28. Churches Together in Britain and Ireland, *Time for Action: Sexual Abuse, the Churches and a New Dawn for Survivors* (London: CTBI, 2002) was a key publication in this regard for the churches.
29. Sue Atkinson, *Breaking the Chains of Abuse: A Practical Guide* (Lion, 2006); Graham Wilmer, *Recovering from the Impact of Sexual Abuse: UTD — a Therapeutic Treatment for Victims of Sexual Abuse* (Wirral: The Lantern Project, 2013); Judith Herman, *Trauma and Recovery: The Aftermath of Violence – from Domestic Abuse to Political Terror* (New York: Basic Books, 1992). The application of the concept of trauma to the effects of abuse as such has been questioned by some; see the discussion of the study by Clancy in Keenan, *Child Sexual Abuse*, pp. xx–xxi.
30. See e.g. Graham Wilmer, *Conspiracy of Faith: Fighting for Justice after Child Abuse* (Cambridge: Lutterworth, 2007).
31. Susan J. Brison, *Aftermath: Violence and the Remaking of a Self* (Princeton: Princeton University Press, 2002), chapter 3, 'Outliving Oneself'.
32. Susan Shooter, *How Survivors of Abuse Relate to God: The Authentic Spirituality of the Annihilated Soul* (Farnham: Ashgate, 2012).
33. Shooter, *Survivors of Abuse*.
34. Brison, *Aftermath*, e.g. p. 102.
35. See for example BBC News report, 'Roman Catholic Church in Scotland Issues Apology for Child Abuse', 18 August 2015, http://www.bbc.co.uk/news/uk-scotland-33959446 (accessed 21/8/2015).
36. Jeremy M. Bergen, *Ecclesial Repentance: The Churches Confront their Sinful Pasts* (London: T & T Clark, 2011), p. 90.
37. Keith W. Carley, *Cambridge Bible Commentary: The Book of the Prophet Ezekiel* (Cambridge: Cambridge University Press, 1974), p. 228.
38. Leslie C. Allen, *Ezekiel 20–48*, Word Bible Commentary Vol. 29 (Texas: Word Books, 1990), p. 165.

39. E.g. Paul Ricoeur, *Critique and Conviction: Conversations with François Azouvi and Marc de Launay*, trans. Kathleen Blimey (New York: Columbia University Press, 1998), pp. 122–3.
40. On this question, see Bash, *Forgiveness and Christian Ethics* (2007), pp. 111–40.
41. See Bergen, *Ecclesial Repentance*, pp. 4 and 264ff.
42. See for instance 'Accepting the Burden of History: Common Declaration of the Bishops' Conferences of the German Federal Republic, of Austria and of Berlin, on the Fiftieth anniversary of the pogroms against the Jewish Community on the night of 9/10 November 1938' (1988), available at https://www.bc.edu/content/dam/files/research_sites/cjl/texts/cjrelations/resources/documents/catholic/burden_of_history.html
43. Bergen, *Ecclesial Repentance*.
44. See *Report of Proceedings 2006 General Synod: February Group of Sessions*, vol. 37.1, pp. 216–36, available at https://www.churchofengland.org/media/40922/rcf06.pdf
45. See for instance the brief summary of perspectives in current ecclesiology on this point in *The Church: Towards a Common Vision*, Faith and Order Paper 214 (Geneva: WCC, 2013), paragraphs 35–6.
46. Bergen, *Ecclesial Repentance*, in particular chapters 4 and 6.
47. Martin Luther, 'Sermon for Easter Sunday 1531', WA 34/1, 276.
48. *Protecting All God's Children*, 8.7.
49. *Promoting a Safe Church*, p. 31.
50. Anthony C. Thiselton, *The First Epistle to the Corinthians* (Grand Rapids: Eerdmans, 2000), p. 390.
51. Thiselton, *Corinthians*, pp. 395–6.
52. Thiselton, *Corinthians*, pp. 397.
53. The Doctrine Commission of the Church of England, *The Mystery of Salvation: The Story of God's Gift* (London: Church House Publishing, 1995), pp. 123–4.
54. For an overview of the background to this, see Carolyn Headley and Bridget Nichols, 'Reconciliation and Restoration', in Paul Bradshaw (ed.), *Companion to Common Worship*, vol. 2 (London: SPCK, 2006), pp. 168–79.
55. Cf. Oliver O'Donovan, *The Desire of the Nations: Rediscovering the Roots of Political Theology* (Cambridge: Cambridge University Press, 1986), pp. 169 and 176–7.
56. Concern about this area has been voiced by the Archbishop of York in his Preface to the *Inquiry into the Church of England's Response to Child Abuse Allegations Made against Robert Waddington* (York: Archbishop of York's Office, 2014), paragraphs 17–18.

57. Keenan, *Child Sexual Abuse*, pp. 162–8.

58. On this subject, see Appendix 1, 'Harmful Theology', in *Responding to Domestic Abuse*, pp. 20–21.

59. Sue Atkinson, *Struggling to Forgive: Moving On From Trauma* (Oxford: Monarch, 2014).

60. W. D. Davies and D. C. Alison, *The Gospel According to Saint Matthew*, Vol. I (Edinburgh: T & T Clark, 1988), p. 610.

61 Thomas Aquinas put it this way: 'the Lord's Prayer is pronounced in the common person of the whole Church: and so if anyone say the Lord's Prayer while unwilling to forgive his neighbour's trespasses, he lies not, although his words do not apply to him personally' (*Summa Theologiae* II–II.83.9, a.3).

62. Lesley Bilinda, 'Remembering Well: The Role of Forgiveness in Remembrance', *Anvil*, 30:2 (September 2014), p. 10.

63. Rowan Williams and Michael Lapsley, 'The Journey Towards Forgiveness: A Dialogue', *The Ecumenical Review*, 66:2 (July 2014), p. 197.

64. Williams and Lapsley, 'Journey Towards Forgiveness', p. 197.

65. Augustine of Hippo, *De mendacio (On Lying)*, e.g. §§ 10 and 15; translation available at http://www.newadvent.org/fathers/1312.htm

66. Williams and Lapsley, 'Journey Towards Forgiveness', p. 211.

67. Cherry, *Healing Agony*.

68. Paul S. Fiddes, 'Restorative Justice and the Theological Dynamic of Forgiveness', *Oxford Journal of Law and Religion*, 5:1 (2016), pp.54–65.

69. While biblical scholars recognize reconciliation as a theme in Paul's writing, there are a variety of views about its significance for his theology; see Corneliu Constantineanu, *The Social Significance of Reconciliation in Paul's Theology: Narrative Readings in Romans* (London and New York: T & T Clark, 2010).

70. Ian Paul, 'Reconciliation in the New Testament', in Andrew Atherstone and Andrew Goddard (eds.), *Good Disagreement? Grace and Truth in a Divided Church* (Oxford: Lion, 2015), pp. 23–41.

71. Steven Tracy, 'Sexual Abuse and Forgiveness', *Journal of Psychology and Theology*, 27:3 (1999), pp. 219–29, especially pp. 223–5. Tracy's 'interpersonal forgiveness' in this article overlaps with how this document understands reconciliation.

72. See Brian Castle, *Reconciliation: The Journey of a Lifetime* (London: SPCK, 2014), pp. 43–64.

73. Mayo, *Limits of Forgiveness*.

74. Fiddes, 'Restorative Justice'.

75. Keenan, *Child Sexual Abuse*, pp. 266–75.

Index

Subject Index

Absalom 48–9, 50–51
absolution, and sin of abuse 13, 63, 74–
    80
abuse:
    and bystanders 49–51, 103–4, 107
    collaboration in 47–9, 111
    and consent 36
    domestic 20, 87, 106, 112–14
    effects on abusers 47–8, 52
    effects on those with responsibility 48–9,
        50, 52, 55–8, 103–4, 107
    effects on victims 11, 41–6, 51–2
    institutional 20
    meaning 11, 32–40
    and power 21, 32, 33–4, 35–6, 37–40,
        46–7, 50, 93, 97
    in Scripture 11, 32, 33–6, 43, 45, 47–9,
        52
    sexual 19, 32, 36, 44
    as sin 10, 11–12, 21, 41–52
    spiritual 20, 99
    theological responses to see theology
    types 19–21
abusers:
    in congregations 71, 81, 112–14
    and deceit 32, 36, 39–40, 47, 51, 79,
        95, 105
    demonization 51
    and forgiveness 10, 12–13, 70–84
    manipulation by 97, 113, 115
    reconciliation with survivors 14, 101, 110
    and repentance 70, 101
    and restorative action 62–3, 75–6, 78–
        9, 84, 95
    risk of re-offending 13, 70, 79, 82
    and self-deceit 13, 36, 70, 79, 115
action, restorative 14, 101
    by the abuser 62–3, 75–6, 78–9, 84, 95
    by the church 108–9
adults, abuse of 20

Amnon, rape of Tamar 33–6, 43, 47–50
anger:
    against abuser 46, 49, 95, 103
    against the church 10, 56, 86, 110
apology:
    collective 59–60, 62–3, 100
    and repentance 12, 54, 55–6, 58–9,
        68–9
Aquinas, St Thomas 95–6, 122 n.61
Augustine of Hippo, St 90, 94, 100

baptism, and sin 72
Bash, Anthony 22
Bathsheba 49
Bilinda, Lesley 91–2, 96, 104
brokenness 45

Canon B 29 76–7
Carley, Keith W. 57
case studies 65–9, 82–4, 98–100, 112–
    14
Cherry, Stephen 22, 95, 119 n.18
children, abuse of 20, 36, 44, 77–8, 98–
    100
church:
    anger against 10, 56, 86, 110
    and forgiveness 95–6
    as holy 59, 60–61, 73
    and ministry of reconciliation 11, 14,
        101–114
    offenders in congregations 71, 81, 112–
        14
    repentance by 10, 12, 54–69, 109
    responsibility of leaders 52, 55–8, 65–9,
        99, 103–4, 107
clergy:
    and child sexual abuse 36, 77–8, 98–
        100
    discipline procedures 58, 68
    as representing the church 61

Index

collaboration in abuse 47–9, 111
confession:
  general 76
  see also absolution
confidentiality 112–13
consent, and abuse 36
context of abuse 20–21

David, King 33–5, 48–51, 52, 57
deceit of abusers 32, 36, 39–40, 47, 51,
  79, 95, 105
demonization of abuser 51
denial, and deceit 51
doctrine, weak 12, 54, 63, 69, 86–7, 116

empathy, and forgiveness 96, 97

forgiveness:
  and the abused 10, 85–100
  and abusers 10, 12–13, 70–84
  divine 88–91, 94, 96, 109, 116
  of institutions 59
  interpersonal 21, 23, 94–7, 105
  as journey 14, 85, 90–93, 108, 116
  and justice 9–10, 12, 14, 25, 29, 54,
    107
  and reconciliation 10–18, 21–4, 113–
    14, 115–16
  and repentance 24, 70, 71–5, 83–4, 95,
    105–6
  and salvation 13, 70, 73, 86
  of the self 23, 82, 98–100
  and sin 9, 42, 70–72, 90, 117
  and survivors 10, 13–14, 85–100, 105
  therapeutic 22–3

The Gospel, Sexual Abuse and the Church
  6, 15, 17–18, 47, 80–81
grace, and repentance 72, 84
Groening, Oskar 106–7

*Guidelines for the Professional Conduct of
  the Clergy* 80
guilt:
  of abusers 48
  collective 59
  victim's feelings of 45, 86–7, 93–4, 97,
    98, 110

harm 43–6, 58, 78–9, 83–4, 102, 115
  and abuse of power 21, 32, 33–4, 35–
    40, 46–7, 50, 93, 97
  caused by inadequate theology 17
  and definition of abuse 11, 32, 34, 36–
    7, 40
  spiritual 20
healing 14, 92–3, 100, 101, 110–111,
  115
holiness, of the church 59, 60–61, 73
humanity, justice and human worth 25–6,
  34, 50

Jones, L. Gregory 22
judgment:
  divine 26, 28, 57, 64
  ecclesial 27
justice 25–9
  eschatological 25, 28–9, 64, 84, 107
  and forgiveness 9–10, 12, 14, 25, 29, 54
  and reconciliation 25, 29
  and repentance 9, 13–14, 95
  restorative 107–9
  as right relations 25–6, 27–8, 29, 34,
    50, 64
  and salvation 64
  temporal 25, 26, 49–50, 57, 79–80, 85,
    101, 106–9, 117
  and the church 11–12, 13, 27–9, 41,
    63–4, 110–111
  and reconciliation 14, 110
  as virtue 25, 27–8, 29, 64

Kor, Eva 106–7

Lambeth Conference 1920, 'Appeal to all
    Christian People' 60
Lapsley, Michael 92–6, 100, 104
Lord's Prayer 87–91, 95–6
Luther, Martin 61

McFadyen, Alistair 44
manipulation by abusers 97, 113, 115
memory, and abuse 11, 41, 46, 93–4, 97,
    100, 110
mercy:
    divine 88–9
    human 89
The Message Bible 88
The Mystery of Salvation 74

objectification of victims 34, 35

Partington, Marian 22
penance 63, 76
pornography 48, 97
power:
    and abuse 21, 32, 33–4, 35–6, 37–40,
        46–7, 50, 93, 97
    relinquishing 105–6, 117
Practice Guidance: Risk Assessment 83
PTSD (post-traumatic stress disorder) 98–
    100

rape:
    and shame 94
    of Tamar 11, 32, 33–6, 43, 45, 47–52
    as weapon of war 51
reconciliation:
    as church's ministry 11, 14, 101–114
    divine–human 102, 114, 116
    and forgiveness 18, 21–4, 113–14,
        115–16

and justice 14, 25, 29, 107–8, 110
and restoration of relationships 9, 14,
    50, 63, 75, 78–81, 84, 101, 104–
    110, 113, 115
sacrament of 74
in theology of Paul 102
Reformation churches, and sin 76–7
relationships:
    divine-human 41, 47, 75, 102, 105
    and inability to trust 46–7
    perversion 42
    restoration 9, 11, 14, 50, 75, 78–81, 84,
        101, 104–110, 113, 115
repentance:
    by churches 10, 12, 54–69, 109
    by individuals 14, 70–80, 105, 111
    collective 59–60, 73
    and forgiveness 24, 70, 71–5, 83–4, 95,
        105–6
    and justice 9, 13–14, 95
    and reconciliation 105–6, 111, 113
    as work of grace 72, 84
    see also action, restorative
restoration:
    and justice 62–3, 107–8
    of relationships 9, 11, 14, 50, 75, 79–
        81, 84, 95, 101, 104–110, 113, 115
Roman Catholic Church:
    and child abuse 56, 76–7
    and ecclesial sin 60
    and justice 27–8
    and sacrament of reconciliation 74, 76–
        7
Rwandan genocide 91–2

safeguarding 66
    and definition of abuse 38–40
    guidance 15, 25
    responsibility for 17–18
    and types of abuse 20

salvation:
  and absolution 76
  and forgiveness 13, 70, 73, 86
  and justice 64
self-deceit 13, 36, 70, 79, 115
Sex Offender Training Programme 82
shame, feelings of 45, 94, 97, 98, 110
Shooter, Susan 46
Shriver, Donald W. 22
sin:
  abuse as 10, 11–12, 21, 41–52
  by the church 59, 60–64, 72–3
  corporate 72–3
  and forgiveness 9, 42, 70–72, 90, 117
  post-baptismal 72
  of those with responsibility 47–8, 56–7
  see also repentance
South Africa:
  Tamar Campaign 33
  Truth and Reconciliation process 23
suicide, and shame 98
survivors:
  and anger against church 10, 56, 86,
    110
  and forgiveness 10, 13–14, 85–100
  and healing 14, 92–3, 100, 101, 110–
    111, 115

listening to 44–5, 50, 56, 68, 85, 86, 110
reconciliation with abusers 14, 101, 110

Tamar, rape 11, 32, 33–6, 43, 45, 47–9,
  52
theology:
  and forgiveness 22, 23–4, 25, 42, 115–
    16
  and justice 25–9
  and power 38–40
  and repentance 60–64
  and responses to abuse 17–18
Thiselton, Anthony C. 73
trauma, abuse as 46, 93
Trible, Phyllis 43
trust:
  betrayal 11, 32, 35–6, 39–40, 46–7, 55,
    103
  manipulation 97, 115
Tutu, Desmond 22, 23, 119 n.12

victims:
  effects of abuse on 11, 41–6
  as survivors 103
Volf, Miroslav 22

Working Together (UK government) 19–20

2588888488

Index of biblical citations

Old Testament

Genesis
38 119 n.16
Judges
19.1 49
21.25 49
2 Samuel
13–14 38, 45, 47–50, 57
13.1-39 11, 32, 33
13.3–5 48
13.8 43
13.12–13 33
13.12 34
13.14 35
13.19 43
13.20 34, 43
13.21 48-9
16.20-23 51
Isaiah
45.21 64
59 64
59.16 64
Lamentations
1.16 43
3.11 43
Ezekiel
34.3 57
34.4 57
34.5 57
34.10 57
34.24-25 57

New Testament

Matthew
3.1–12 72
3.8 75
6.9-15 87-8
6.12 89
6.14-15 87, 88
6.33 64
7.9 115
11.20 59
12.45 59
16.2 89
18.15-20 72
18.23-35 89
18.35 88
Mark
1.4 72
2.5-7 71
Luke
1.77 72
3.1–3 72
7.41-50 91
10.31-3 59
11.2-4 87-8
11.11-24 71
11.32 59
13.3-5 59
19 75
19.1-10 105
19.1-9 71
John
1.5 117
8.1–11 105
8.32 115
Acts
2.38 72
9.1-19 105
22.6-21 105
1 Corinthians
5.1-5 73, 75, 109
5.2 73
5.5 73
2 Corinthians
1.20 64
2.5-11 72
5.18-21 102
5.21 96, 102
Ephesians
2.14-19 110
1 Timothy
5.20 72
Hebrews
10.26-31 72
1 Peter
2.14 26
3.13 28
Revelation
13.8 116

127

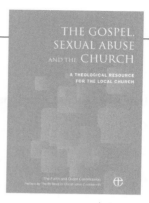

The Gospel, Sexual Abuse and the Church

A Theological Resource for the Local Church

The Faith and Order Commission

With a Foreword by The Rt Revd Christopher Cocksworth, Chair of The Faith and Order Commission

The Gospel, Sexual Abuse and the Church has been written by the Faith and Order Commission of the Church of England in response to a request from the lead bishop for safeguarding for theological material that complements the work of the National Safeguarding Team on policy and training.

It has been approved for publication and commended for study by the House of Bishops.

The Gospel, Sexual Abuse and the Church is intended to be used by those with responsibility for teaching and preaching in the Church of England, including clergy and licensed lay ministers, and those with specific responsibilities for safeguarding training. The three main sections provide material that can be used for training sessions and study days, with groups such as a PCC or Church Council, a ministry team, or a discussion group.

Each section includes suggested quotations for reflection, discussion questions and a 'Bible focus'.

Available from your local Christian bookseller or:
Online: www.chpublishing.co.uk
Phone: 01603 785 925
E-mail: orders@norwichbooksandmusic.co.uk